Biomedical Ethics

OPPOSING
VIEWPOINTS®
DIGESTS

Biomedical Ethics

TERRY O'NEILL

$$\left[\begin{array}{c} \textbf{OPPOSING} \\ \textbf{VIEWPOINTS}^{\textregistered} \\ \textbf{DIGESTS} \end{array}\right]$$

Greenhaven Press, Inc., San Diego, California

Library of Congress Cataloging-in-Publication Data

O'Neill, Terry, 1949–
    Biomedical ethics / Terry O'Neill.
        p.   cm. — (Opposing viewpoints digests)
    Includes bibliographical references and index.
    ISBN 1-56510-874-4 (pbk. : alk. paper) — ISBN 1-56510-875-2
(lib. bdg. : alk. paper)
    1. Medical ethics—Juvenile literature. 2. Bioethics—Juvenile
literature. [1. Medical ethics. 2. Bioethics.] I. Title. II. Series.
R724.063   1999
174'.2—dc21   98-37239
                                                                                 CIP
                                                                                 AC

Cover Photo: Copyright © 1997 PhotoDisc
AP/Wide World: 11, 21, 27, 41, 54, 75
Sinclair Stammers/Science Photo Library: 64
United States Holocaust Memorial Museum/
Yad Vashem Archives, Courtesy of USHMM Photo Archives: 32

©1999 by Greenhaven Press, Inc.
PO Box 289009, San Diego, CA 92198-9009

Printed in the U.S.A.

CONTENTS

FOREWORD

The only way in which a human being can make some approach to knowing the whole of a subject is by hearing what can be said about it by persons of every variety of opinion and studying all modes in which it can be looked at by every character of mind. No wise man ever acquired his wisdom in any mode but this.

—John Stuart Mill

Today, young adults are inundated with a wide variety of points of view on an equally wide spectrum of subjects. Often overshadowing traditional books and newspapers as forums for these views are a host of broadcast, print, and electronic media, including television news and entertainment programs, talk shows, and commercials; radio talk shows and call-in lines; movies, home videos, and compact discs; magazines and supermarket tabloids; and the increasingly popular and influential Internet.

For teenagers, this multiplicity of sources, ideas, and opinions can be both positive and negative. On the one hand, a wealth of useful, interesting, and enlightening information is readily available virtually at their fingertips, underscoring the need for teens to recognize and consider a wide range of views besides their own. As Mark Twain put it, "It were not best that we should all think alike; it is difference of opinion that makes horse races." On the other hand, the range of opinions on a given subject is often too wide to absorb and analyze easily. Trying to keep up with, sort out, and form personal opinions from such a barrage can be daunting for anyone, let alone young people who have not yet acquired effective critical judgment skills.

Moreover, to the task of evaluating this assortment of impersonal information, many teenagers bring firsthand experience of serious and emotionally charged social and health problems, including divorce, family violence, alcoholism and drug abuse, rape, unwanted pregnancy, the spread of AIDS, and eating disorders. Teens are often forced to deal with these problems before they are capable of objective opinion based on reason and judgment. All too often, teens' response to these deep personal issues is impulsive rather than carefully considered.

Greenhaven Press's Opposing Viewpoints Digests are designed to aid in examining important current issues in a way that develops critical thinking and evaluating skills. Each book presents thought-provoking argument and stimulating debate on a single issue. By examining an issue from many different points of view, readers come to realize its complexity and acknowledge the validity of opposing opinions. This insight is especially helpful in writing reports, research papers, and persuasive essays, when students must competently address common objections and controversies related to their topic. In addition, examination of the diverse mix of opinions in each volume challenges readers to question their own strongly held opinions and assumptions. While the point of such examination is not to change readers' minds, examining views that oppose their own will certainly deepen their own knowledge of the issue and help them realize exactly why they hold the opinion they do.

The Opposing Viewpoints Digests offer a number of unique features that sharpen young readers' critical thinking and reading skills. To assure an appropriate and consistent reading level for young adults, all essays in each volume are written by a single author. Each essay heavily quotes readable primary sources that are fully cited to allow for further research and documentation. Thus, primary sources are introduced in a context to enhance comprehension.

In addition, each volume includes extensive research tools. A section containing relevant source material includes interviews, excerpts from original research, and the opinions of prominent spokespersons. A "facts about" section allows students to peruse relevant facts and statistics; these statistics are also fully cited, allowing students to question and analyze the credibility of the source. Two bibliographies, one for young adults and one listing the author's sources, are also included; both are annotated to guide student research. Finally, a comprehensive index allows students to scan and locate content efficiently.

Greenhaven's Opposing Viewpoints Digests, like Greenhaven's higher level and critically acclaimed Opposing Viewpoints Series, have been developed around the concept that an awareness and appreciation for the complexity of seemingly simple issues is particularly important in a democratic society. In a democracy, the common good is often, and very appropriately, decided by open debate of widely varying views. As one of our democracy's greatest advocates, Thomas Jefferson, observed, "Difference of opinion leads to inquiry, and inquiry to truth." It is to this principle that Opposing Viewpoints Digests are dedicated.

The World of Biomedical Technology Today

Today's technology is creating possibilities no one could have imagined only a few decades ago. Science has made possible human space flight, moon landings, and launches of vehicles capable of photographing and performing sophisticated tests on distant planets. Teleportation (sending something from one place to another in a flash, through no visible means but rather on a molecular level) used to be the stuff of science fiction and *Star Trek*, but today corporations such as IBM and other scientific research organizations have actually taken the first step to make this a reality. Thanks to computers and the Internet, people can instantaneously exchange their thoughts with people anyplace in the world—or out of it. Your grandparents—even your parents—probably did not dream that these modern realities would occur in their lifetime.

In the world of medicine, advances have been just as spectacular. Scientists have almost entirely eliminated a number of diseases like tuberculosis, diphtheria, and polio that killed millions of people only a few decades ago. People who would have died of heart diseases a generation ago are surviving because of advances in pharmacology (the science of drugs), organ repair and transplantation, and end-of-life care. People with conditions that prevented them from having children in the past have many options to help them today. These are all accomplishments of scientists working in the biomedical sciences.

Biomedical Ethics

Biomedical science involves the use of biological materials (that is, living matter, plant or animal) in the field of medicine. Those materials are used to improve old ways and create new ways of enhancing human health. It includes new and improved medicines created from both biological and nonbiological materials; new ways of aiding people who have lost the use of an organ or a limb; methods of prolonging life and health for the aging; preventing inherited disease; and much, much more.

Ethics involves right and wrong. Lisa Yount, author of *Issues in Biomedical Ethics*, writes that "ethical problems arise when two or more values suggest conflicting actions or conflicting judgments about a particular action."[1] For example, one controversial area of biomedicine involves the use of animal organs as replacement parts for humans. A procedure of great promise is transplantation of the pig heart. Surprisingly, pig anatomy is very similar to human anatomy, so scientists believe that they might successfully replace certain human parts with pig parts. If they can keep the human body from rejecting a pig heart, for example, doctors would have a practical, economical, and plentiful supply of hearts to transplant to people with damaged, diseased, or defective ones. Since heart disease is the biggest killer of Americans, many American researchers hope they are on the way to solving the problem of the body's natural rejection of foreign tissue.

The benefit of this procedure is evident. But the issue is not a simple one. Many people object to the use of animal parts in humans on ethical grounds. Some say it is wrong to exploit animals in this way. Others say the practice violates the laws of nature. So an ethical dilemma (problem) results. Is using pig hearts to replace human ones a good thing? Bioethicists attempt to answer this kind of question.

The advances we see in biomedical science today have almost all come about in the last few decades of the twentieth century, and the changes have come fast and furious—in some cases, too fast for people to know how to respond to them. All technical advances, no matter how exciting and beneficial, bring with them troubling questions. Bioethicists try to help people consider the implications of new technology and decide how to respond.

Issues

Biomedical ethical questions usually revolve around six main issues:

- Autonomy, or the right of individuals to make their own decisions

- Personhood, or what it means to be a human being

- Beneficence, or doing good to others

- Nonharm, or not doing bad to others

- Justice, or being fair to all

- Consequences, or the effect of the chosen action

Here's how these issues might come up in one biomedical case.

In 1996, doctors told former baseball great Mickey Mantle that his liver was damaged beyond repair. If Mantle's life was to be prolonged, he would need a liver transplant. Mantle's liver was in such terrible condition in part because of the effects of chronic alcoholism. Alcohol abuse has long been proven to destroy the liver, and most adults know this. Mantle could only receive a new liver if a donated liver was transplanted from someone who died, and there is a national waiting list for that procedure. Typically, a person in need of a new liver must wait anywhere from a few weeks to more than a year. Mantle, however, underwent a successful transplant within two days of being told that he needed one.

Autonomy: If the person whose liver was given to Mantle *chose* to donate the organ, autonomy was maintained. But often this is not what happens. Often, people do not get

Mickey Mantle (pictured) ducked the national waiting list for organ transplants and received a new liver within two days of his diagnosis.

around to telling anyone whether or not they want to donate organs, so the person's family or, rarely, hospital personnel decide whether to "harvest" the organ. ("Harvest" is the term most often used to describe the act of taking an organ from one person to use in another.) This decision might be the same decision the dying person would have made, but sometimes certainty is not possible. Bioethicists have helped guide governments and medical institutions to find methods of making sure it is the donor's choice to give the organ.

Personhood: An issue that bioethicists and others debate is what it means to be human. When it comes to organ transplants, for example, some people say that they are unnatural. They go against God's laws or nature's laws. Others say personhood is not important in the transplant issue. It is more important to heal a person than to worry about whether using someone else's organs makes us less human.

Beneficence: In Mickey Mantle's case, the person whose liver Mantle received made a beneficent organ donation. But an ethical issue might come up if, for example, the donor or the donor's family did not really want the donor to be "mutilated," to have pieces removed from his or her body.

Nonharm: Mantle was not harmed by gaining the new liver, and the donor was not harmed if he or she wanted to donate the organ, but what about the people who had been waiting for a liver much longer than Mantle? Were they harmed?

Justice: Justice is in part a combination of beneficence and nonharm. It is an issue that frequently comes up in biomedical ethics because justice is so difficult to achieve. Ideally, the ethical choice is fair to all, but in reality that is almost impossible. Nevertheless, it is important that justice be considered as part of the decision-making process. In Mantle's case, most people would probably argue that justice was not done; Mantle did not wait a normal amount of time, and because he was in effect moved to the head of the line, all the other patients had to wait longer, and someone at the bottom of the waiting list might even have died as a result.

But who should determine what is just when it comes to waiting lists? Until May 1998, donated organs were first offered to a waiting list in the same geographic area as the donor. This meant that waiting lists were short in some areas with high rates of donation and long in others. In May 1998 the U.S. government changed the rules so that organs would be given to the person deemed most sick, no matter where in the country he or she lives. In one sense, this seems more fair. But some have argued that the sickest people are also the least likely to survive a transplant, so perhaps the organs should go to those who are likely to live the longest with the new organ.

It is also true that people in need of transplants are often not listed at all if they have no medical insurance coverage or money to pay for the transplant and the other expenses involved for care and medicine. Some would say this is unjust, but others point out that if the poor are allowed onto waiting lists, the rest of us will have to pay their bills and that would not be just either.

Another factor in the Mantle case is that Mantle's liver damage was, at least in part, his own fault. If he had not abused alcohol, his liver might very well have stayed healthy. An ethical issue that often comes up in cases like this is whether it is just to donate organs that are in great demand to someone whose own behavior has caused the damage, especially if he or she is likely to continue the abuse that damaged the organ, thereby leading to the destruction of the transplanted one as well. Some would argue that alcoholics should not be given new livers; new organs should only go to those who did not cause their own illness. Others counter that alcoholism itself is a disease and that alcoholics cannot control their drinking and therefore should not be punished for it.

Consequences: Bioethicists have to consider the effects of the choice that is made. In the Mantle case, for example, a bioethicist might be concerned that Mantle's early organ transplant would set a precedent (a decision that will act as an example and model for future decisions); that is, it would establish a basis for giving preference to other baseball players, celebrities, or rich people.

Another term for this is "slippery slope." People who use this term think of a particular situation as being at the top of a slope, or hill; if the consequences of one situation lead to another situation and yet another, ever more dire, they are likened to sliding down a slippery slope. So, in the Mantle example, one celebrity (Mantle) is at the top of the slope. If his case means other celebrities get organs first, at the expense of noncelebrities, the situation is a slippery slope.

Bioethicists look at a wide range of cases to try to help the government or private groups or individuals form ethical views and make decisions about biomedical issues on the basis of ethical considerations.

The Human Genome Project

One of the most important events in the history of biomedical ethics was the inauguration of the Human Genome Project. This project has led to many controversial biomedical advances; consequently, it has also generated numerous ethical debates.

The Human Genome Project (HGP) is a fifteen-year international project in which scientists from at least eighteen countries are working to identify and map the entire human genome, a group of sixty thousand to eighty thousand genes. Genes determine all of our physical characteristics and some of our psychological characteristics as well. Some scientists believe that behavior is also influenced, if not caused, by genes.

The sixty thousand to eighty thousand human genes consist of DNA, the nucleic acid that composes proteins, the building blocks of biological matter. DNA consists of spiraling sequences of four similar chemicals, called bases, "that are repeated millions or billions of times throughout a genome," states a publication of the U.S. Department of Energy (DOE). The DOE is one of the two agencies managing U.S. participation in the Human Genome Project. (The other is the National Institutes of Health.) "The human genome . . . has 3 billion pairs of bases,"[2] continues the publication; the HGP scientists are trying to identify the long strings of pairs that are defined as genes. The particular order of the bases and the pairs determines the organism's physical and many other qualities.

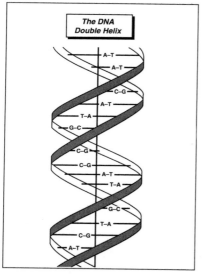

In 1990, scientists began the Human Genome Project, an aggressive effort to establish the purpose of each gene in the human body. Genes are coded in DNA, as represented by this illustration.

The project, officially begun in 1990 and ultimately expected to cost more than $3 billion, is unique in its degree of international cooperation. All contributions made by all the scientists working on the project are fed into a database accessible to scientists all over the world.

The researchers are also studying the genomes of a number of other species so they can be compared with the human genome to discover what makes humans different from pigs, for example. The genetic code of less complex organisms can also be unraveled more quickly. Simpler organisms, or living things, not only have smaller genomes (the fruit fly, for example, has only about 165 million bases), but shorter life spans, so genetic changes can be observed more quickly than in humans. To see how changes in a gene affect a human, scientists have to wait at least one generation—until the person's children are born—and perhaps more. This takes decades. But many generations of fruit flies can be studied during a period as short as a month. Since the principles, if not the exact workings, of genetic change are the same in fruit flies and humans, some knowledge about human genetics can be learned by what happens to the fruit flies. Other organisms whose genomes are being studied include the *E. coli* bacteria, yeast, roundworm, and mouse.

Surprisingly, geneticists say that all mammals have almost identical genes. "Gene for gene, we are very similar to mice," says Lisa Stubbs of Lawrence Livermore National Laboratory in California, one of the major sites of HGP research. "The differences between mice and humans are not in the number of genes we each carry but in the structure of genes and the activities of their protein products. . . . What really matters is that around 100,000 very subtle changes add together to make quite different organisms."[3] HGP scientists hope that by comparing the genes of different species, they will be able to tell what these "very subtle changes" are that make the difference between human and mouse. In fact, a long-range goal of the world's genome projects is to map the genomes of all living creatures in hopes of not only greater understanding, but the ability to do some genetic "mix-and-matching" to create new foods, medicines, and other products that will benefit humanity.

Benefits of the Human Genome Project

The major goals of studying the human genome include understanding the very nature of life itself; being able to compare the genetic structures of healthy and sick people and through the differences discovered, find solutions to disease; learning to manipulate genes to create adaptations that will improve human health (for example, scientists today are using gene manipulation to breed cows that will make vaccine-laden milk so vaccinations can be avoided); learning how to identify in advance people with a genetic predisposition to certain diseases so that preventive treatment can be initiated at the earliest possible stage; developing profitable "bioproducts," such as disease-free food products; and actually altering the genetic makeup of disease-prone people so that they will no longer be susceptible to inherited diseases.

But as in most research, these and other benefits of the HGP come alongside potential dangers as well. Many people have serious concerns about the HGP. They think this kind of research raises important ethical issues. A very basic issue is the nature of the project itself. Is it right for humans to seek to know the secrets of life?

Many ethical questions concern more specific aspects of the research. For example, scientists who discover a new gene sequence, a key to a disease such as cancer or Alzheimer's disease, are patenting their discoveries. To patent something is to file an official claim of ownership. The owner of the patented item has the right to sell it, or to license it to others to use, or even to prevent others from using it. So, for example, if a scientist discovers a genetic secret that is the key to ending lung cancer, he or she might patent it. Then anybody who wanted to take advantage of the discovery—doctors looking for new ways to treat their patients, pharmaceutical companies who want to sell drugs based on the discovery—would have to get the permission of the patent owner. Objectors feel that life and its mechanisms should belong to no individual or company, but rather be shared knowledge used to provide benefits to as many people as possible.

Another ethical concern is that the HGP discoveries will be used not only therapeutically (to help those who are sick) but cosmetically (to improve those who are already well). Hypothetically, the discovery of the genetic secret to improving the intelligence of those who would otherwise be retarded might be considered therapeutic. But to increase the intelligence of someone already of average or above-average intelligence would probably be considered cosmetic. Ethicists are concerned that the availability of this type of treatment would undermine human individuality and also make discrimination more widespread. If it were possible to make geniuses of everyone with sufficient resources, would society discriminate against those who were not geniuses? Carried to the extreme, would the type of eugenic cleansing occur that took place in Nazi Germany? (During World War II, the Nazis made an effort to wipe out all those who did not fit an idealized profile. The retarded, Jews, and the physically disabled were all considered inferior and expendable, and millions of people in these categories were killed by the Nazis. Some ethicists worry that this kind of genocide could happen again.)

RUNAWAY TRAIN

One more ethical issue raised by the HGP is cloning. Cloning is creating a new organism from the cell of another, single organism rather than a pair of "parent" cells. Then both organisms are completely identical biologically. While cloning has been the stuff of science fiction for many years, only recently has genetic research turned this fantasy into a reality. In the future, in theory, it would be possible to make an exact duplicate of you.

Ethicists are worried about more than the duplication of people, however. For example, some researchers are working on taking a cell from a human liver and trying to grow a new, identical liver in a laboratory. This kind of cloning would be beneficial to people who need a new liver, but it also conjures up images of laboratories that are like biological gardens— livers growing here, hearts there, and so on. Would this be an ethical use of technology?

These are only a few examples of the many kinds of ethical issues that have resulted from the amazing advances in medical science. As scientists continue to learn more, we will have more decisions to make. The more we know about these issues and about our own values, the more ready we will be to participate in this exciting new world.

1.   Lisa Yount, *Issues in Biomedical Ethics.* San Diego: Lucent Books, 1997, p. 12.

2.   "Human Genome Project Information," U.S. Department of Energy. On-line. Internet. Available at http://www.ornl.gov/TechResources/HumanGenome/home.html, June 21, 1998.

3.   Quoted in "Human Genome Project Frequently Asked Questions," U.S. Department of Energy. On-line. Internet. Available at http://www.ornl.gov/TechResources/HumanGenome/home.html, June 21, 1998.

CHAPTER 1

Medical Testing and Research

"Today many diseases are virtually extinct because of cures discovered through scientists' work with animal subjects."

Animal Medical Research Is Necessary

"Virtually every major medical advance for both humans and animals has been achieved through research using animal models and testing,"[1] writes former U.S. surgeon general C. Everett Koop. Koop and others accurately point out that if scientists had not been able to use animals in their research, they would not have discovered treatments and cures for an array of diseases that have killed huge numbers of people, sometimes wiping out most of a city, region, or ethnic group. Today many diseases are virtually extinct because of cures discovered through scientists' work with animal subjects.

Past Medicine

Years ago, the scientific method of devising an experiment to test a theory, then analyzing test results to see if the theory holds up, then experimenting again, was not widely used in medicine. People relied on folk remedies—traditional treatments that were handed down from generation to generation. Unfortunately, we know today that some of these remedies resulted in more harm than cures. For example, one folk remedy was bloodletting. By making small cuts on the patient's skin and allowing blood to flow, the medical practitioner believed, the sickness would flow from the body as well. But

Surgeon General C. Everett Koop answers questions about smoking at a Washington conference. Animal testing has made it possible to measure the harm smoking does to the human body.

in some cases, the patient did not get better; he or she died from loss of blood.

In other cases, drugs were discovered that seemed to have great promise, so doctors and patients used them indiscriminately. In the eighteenth century, for example, wealthy people ingested bits of silver to keep themselves healthy. They didn't make the connection when their skin developed a permanent blue cast and they died of liver failure caused by silver poisoning.

In still other cases drugs known to alleviate certain problems had harmful side effects that weren't detected until too late, sometimes years later. Thalidomide is an example. This drug was known to prevent or reduce nausea and anxiety, so it was given to many pregnant women in the 1950s and early 1960s. Only too late was it discovered that the drug also caused severe birth defects.

In addition to problems caused by ignorance were the tragedies caused by charlatans, the so-called snake-oil salesmen who simply took an inert or useless substance and asserted that it could heal.

All of these problems led to strict Food and Drug Administration (FDA) regulation of all substances sold as medicines, including thorough testing before the drug enters the market. The tests progress from laboratory work, to use on animals, and finally to tests on humans. They are tested on animals before humans to spare human lives. Necessarily, this means that some animals die during the experimentation. Ernst Knobil, former president of the American Physiological Society, uses the example of polio vaccine to show why this is essential. Polio, a devastating disease that causes paralysis and other problems, has been virtually eliminated because of the vaccine that was developed in the 1950s and widely administered. Knobil states:

> In the testing of polio vaccine, where a small error could paralyze hundreds of children, I would not want to have my child or grandchild inoculated with a product that had not been submitted to the most rigorous testing procedures, which include administration of the vaccine to . . . monkeys and the careful examination of their brains and spinal cords afterwards.[2]

Animal Testing

Although animals and humans don't always react in the same way to drugs, many animals react similarly enough that scientists can predict how the substances will work on humans. As Richard McCourt writes in *Discover* magazine, "Any little mammal will provide a reasonable analogy to a human. . . . Our hemoglobin, cell membranes, and many enzymes are so similar that what's true for one is often true for the other."[3]

There are several areas in which animal experimentation is particularly valuable today besides drug development. For instance, animals can be used to test surgical procedures. Researchers at England's National Institute for Medical Research are using rats to try to discover how spinal cords can be regrown. Spinal cord injuries are among the most tragic accidents people suffer. Diving into an unfamiliar body of water and striking one's head on a rock, being thrown from a horse or motorcycle, and many other types of accidents can cause spinal cord injuries that involve permanent paralysis.

The English scientists are finding that it may be possible to regrow nerve axons that make up the spinal cord. The scientists have transplanted protective nerve cells from rats' olfactory systems, reports Phil Berardelli in *Insight on the News* on October 27, 1997. The transplanted cells sheathed the axons and soon the rats' axons regenerated. If the scientists can perfect this work they may be able to offer a new chance at a normal life to people like actor Christopher Reeve, a quadriplegic since being thrown from his horse.

Researchers at the University of Connecticut have successfully used heat-shocked proteins to treat cancers in mice, and scientists at Huntingdon Laboratories in New Jersey have worked with dogs to test drugs that could prevent osteoporosis, a disease that weakens the bones, making them brittle and susceptible to fractures. Other scientists are using monkeys to try to find a cure for AIDS, rats and mice to study Alzheimer's, and roundworms to try to discover ways to slow human aging. Experimental animals are even traveling into space. Among the first "astronauts" were chimpanzees and dogs, and a small colony of rats flew aboard the space shuttle *Columbia* on its spring 1998 flight. The scientists aboard the spacecraft dissected the rats' brains to discover how the nervous system reacts to weightlessness, vital knowledge for the future of the space program.

No Animals in Research?

Some people say that medical advances can be accomplished without the use of animals. These critics describe alternative means of experimentation. For example, some kinds of testing can be done with computer simulations. But these aren't sufficient. "We're dealing with a scientifically uneducated public which is eager to believe that there is an alternative to animal research,"[4] says Frankie Trull, president of the Foundation for Biomedical Research (FBR) in Washington, D.C. She argues that animal research is absolutely essential, and she points to major medical discoveries in the areas of breast cancer, Parkinson's disease, and heart disease as proof of the importance of animal research.

Another common objection to using animals in research is that they suffer. But since the 1966 Animal Welfare Act, the government has kept a very close watch on laboratories and how they use animals. There are strict regulations regarding experimental animals' comfort (food, water, and living quarters) and their treatment in the experiments themselves. Before these regulations, admittedly, there were abuses. But now every effort is made to ensure that animals don't feel pain, aren't permanently disabled, and aren't needlessly killed.

In fact, the alternative research methods that have been devised have actually cut down on the number of animals used. The FBR says that in the past twenty years, the number of animals used in research has declined by 20 to 50 percent. Before 1970, "as many as 50 million animals were used each year. . . . The current number . . . is 17–22 million,"[5] the majority of which are rats and mice. Researchers are always looking for ways to make their science better and to avoid harming any living creature as they work.

Scientists are not eager to expend animal life, but they know that this is the best way to assure that drugs and other medical treatments are safe for humans. "We're trying to make animal life, human life, and plant life better,"[6] says Karen Sokol, a veterinarian who conducts experiments on animals.

1.   Quoted in "Battle over Animal Rights," *Current Events*, December 9, 1996, p. 2A.

2.   Quoted in Lawrence Pringle, *The Animal Rights Controversy*. San Diego: Harcourt Brace Jovanovich, 1989, p. 71.

3.   Richard McCourt, "Model Patients," *Discover*, August 1990, p. 36.

4.   Quoted in Leslie Ann Horvitz, "Are Animal Advocates Biting the Hand of Dedicated Docs?" *Insight on the News*, May 19, 1997, p. 40.

5.   "Battle over Animal Rights," *Current Events*, December 9, 1996, p. 4A.

6.   Quoted in "Battle over Animal Rights," *Current Events*, December 9, 1996, p. 3A.

"[Animals] are subjected to unbelievably cruel treatment in the name of science."

Animal Medical Research Is Not Necessary

"Drugs react differently in humans than they do in animals," says Dr. Ron Alison. "It's like putting parts from a Ford into a Sherman tank."[1] Alison doesn't believe it's necessary to use animals in medical research. In fact, he thinks it may lead to wrong scientific conclusions.

Dr. Neal D. Barnard, president of Physicians Committee for Responsible Medicine, agrees. He points out examples where the Food and Drug Administration's (FDA) rigid testing regulations were followed, with laboratory, animal, and human tests, and yet the tested products were still discovered to have damaging flaws. One prominent example is the diet drug popularly called Phen-Fen. It was released as a boon to obese people who could not lose weight any other way. Six million Americans used the drug before it was discovered that it caused severe and permanent heart damage in many patients. Phen-Fen was withdrawn from the market.

Barnard points to another drug prescribed for hepatitis B, a severe liver disease. The drug was found safe for monkeys, dogs, and mice, but after it was approved for sale, even taken as prescribed, it caused pancreatitis (an inflammation of the pancreas), nerve damage, and liver and kidney failure in humans. In fact, he says, a 1990 report from the U.S. General Accounting Office reported that more than half of the new drugs that passed all animal tests and were allowed into the marketplace had to be recalled or relabeled "because of adverse reactions that lead to hospitalization, disability, and death."[2]

The problem of translating the results of animal experiments to their efficacy on humans isn't limited to drugs. An article in *Current Events* points out that the artificial test dummies presently used in automobile crash tests give much more reliable previews of what happens to humans involved in auto accidents than did the poor monkeys used previously.

Why don't animals provide the right kind of data to do efficient medical testing? Well, as Barnard says, "Rats, dogs, and cats don't look like us, they don't have the same spectrum of diseases, and they don't test like us." He adds, "There are enormous differences between species in the speed at which drugs are absorbed and the ways drugs are carried in the blood, broken apart in the liver, and excreted, not to mention the differences in how drugs attach to cells and do their work."[3] Pet owners know that chocolate, a delectable treat for humans, can make a dog or cat deathly ill. Animals' systems simply aren't the same as humans', so we shouldn't be surprised that medical tests aren't going to turn out the same on an animal subject as they do on people.

Animal-Test Evils

One of the most common complaints about animal testing is not its unreliability, but the inhumane treatment the animal test subjects receive. Test animals are kept in small cages in labs instead of being able to freely enjoy the environment around them. Many animals have little contact with humans or other animals, contrary to a basic need for almost all warm-blooded animals. And they are subjected to unbelievably cruel treatment in the name of science.

People for the Ethical Treatment of Animals (PETA) is one of several organizations working to eliminate animal-based research and to improve the lives of the animals currently in laboratories. Periodically they conduct undercover investigations and then release their reports to the public. In the spring of 1997, PETA investigated Huntingdon Laboratories in New Jersey. Huntingdon is an independent lab that does work for companies like Colgate-Palmolive. PETA's president, Ingrid Newkirk, reported that the lab's experiments for Colgate included "the four basic tests for products . . . shove it in the animal's throat, poke it in the eye, shove it up the nose, and rub it in abraded skin."[4] This description is not exaggerated; much animal experimentation depends on testing a product on raw membranes to get the most noticeable reactions.

Newkirk also said the investigation showed that dogs were to have their legs broken as part of an experiment for another pharmaceutical company. Monkeys "were improperly anesthetized while technicians ripped out their organs"[5] in still another study.

Activists rally outside Procter & Gamble to protest the company's practice of animal testing.

"It's a hidden world of suffering in the laboratory," said Newkirk. "A normal person would be appalled at the disrespect, let alone the pain"[6] of the animals.

Horrifying as these conditions are, some animal rights advocates describe even worse treatment. There are those who say the 1966 Animal Welfare Act ended the abuse of animals in research laboratories, but this is not true.

Good Alternatives

Fortunately, there are good alternatives to animal experimentation. People do want to know that when they use a medical product they are going to be safe, and there are ways—better ways than using animals—to assure this.

One alternative is computer simulation. With all the advances that have been made in computer technology, it is possible to simulate the effects of drugs, to allow student doctors to practice surgery, and to enable researchers to do many other things in the medical field. Neal Barnard points out that "before a drug is even manufactured, its molecular structure is subjected to complex computer analysis, looking not only at whether it will do what it is supposed to do, but also at what side effects it could cause."[7] Computer simulation makes it possible to determine whether an antibiotic will be ineffective against certain bacteria, for example.

Researchers can also do cellular tests. That is, they can take actual human cells, from a liver, for example, and test the drug's interactions with the cells. Barnard says that "safety tests with human cells were [proven] more accurate at predicting toxicity [poisonousness] than tests done on live animals."[8] An additional benefit: Cell tests are cheaper. There's no animal to feed and shelter every day.

End Animal Experimentation

It's clear that since animal testing is an inhumane process, its results are unreliable, and effective alternative experimental methods are available, medical use of animal testing should be banned.

1. Quoted in "Battle over Animal Rights," *Current Events*, December 9, 1996, p. 4A.

2. Neal D. Barnard, "What Works for Animals Isn't Necessarily Good for Humans," Knight-Ridder/Tribune News Service, January 14, 1998.

3. Barnard, "What Works for Animals Isn't Necessarily Good for Humans."

4. Quoted in Gina Kolata, "Rights vs. Research: Question of Ethics," New York Times News Service, April 1, 1998.

5. Kolata, "Rights vs. Research."

6. Quoted in Kolata, "Rights vs. Research."

7. Barnard, "What Works for Animals Isn't Necessarily Good for Humans."

8. Barnard, "What Works for Animals Isn't Necessarily Good for Humans."

"Researchers [are required to] do everything possible to protect [human] subjects from harm and to stop the experiment if there is evidence of harmful effects."

Human Research Subjects Are Adequately Protected

The Food and Drug Administration (FDA) is a department of the U.S. government. It is responsible for determining which drugs and medical treatments are safe for doctors to use on their patients. Before any new drug or treatment is approved, it must go through a very rigid testing procedure. First the drug is tested in the laboratory. Next it is tested on animals. Finally it is tested on human patients. These human tests, or experiments, are called clinical trials. Altogether, the research and testing phase of drug development may take ten years or more.

Researchers approach all the steps very carefully. By the time they get to human subjects, they may be fairly certain the drug will do what it is supposed to do. But they must test it on humans just to be sure. Most drugs do not act exactly the same on humans as they do on animals. Also, clinical trials are conducted to see if there are any side effects that show up only after prolonged use.

"The word 'experimental' may frighten people," says Lawrence Friedman, M.D., of the Clinical Trials Branch of the National Heart, Blood, and Lung Institute in Bethesda, Maryland. "But by the time a treatment gets to the point where humans are used, short-term safety and effectiveness are established. What we're looking for at this stage is evidence that the new treatment has advantages over existing, approved therapies."[1]

Testing drugs on human subjects is absolutely essential. It is better to test something on a relatively small number of people under very strict controls than to give the drug to huge numbers of patients and only find out by accident that there are unexpected, undesirable results. "Medical advances would not occur without clinical trials,"[2] says Dorothy Cirelli of the National Institutes of Health.

In the Past

Years ago, many new drugs and treatments were given to patients without any systematic testing. Some examples, reports Dr. Eugene Passamani, are "gastric freezing for peptic ulcer disease [and] radiation therapy for acne."[3] Today we know these are very extreme and even dangerous treatments for those health problems.

Additionally, years ago if research *was* done, human subjects were often put at great risk. Sometimes researchers did not even tell people that they were research subjects. Sometimes the researchers had no clear idea what a drug would do—that is why they were testing it.

Today, however, researchers have very strict rules they must follow, rules that protect human subjects. These rules actually came about as a result of the Nazi experiments during World War II. After the war, selected high-ranking Nazis were tried as war criminals. Their trials took place in Nuremberg, Germany. Revelations of horrific abuse in the name of research shocked people. The medical world was determined that this kind of abuse would not happen again, and they developed a code of ethics for working with human research subjects, called the Nuremberg Code. Its ten guidelines include requirements that subjects must be told they are being used in research and they must voluntarily agree to par-

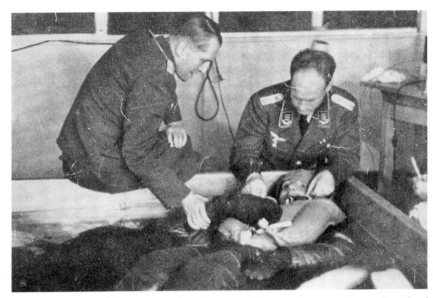

New international laws governing the use of humans in experimental medical procedures came about as a result of the Nuremberg Trials, which exposed the Nazis' grisly human experiments to the world. Here, a prisoner in Dachau concentration camp is dunked in ice water to test the effects of hypothermia.

ticipate. Additionally, the researchers must do everything possible to protect the subjects from harm and to stop the experiment if there is evidence of harmful effects.

Since 1947 when the Nuremberg Code was established, the United States and other countries have updated the guidelines, but the ideas stay the same: The welfare of the research subjects is most important.

Assuring Safety

Today, almost all medical research involving human patients requires the approval of an institutional review board (IRB). This is a group of doctors and scientists who carefully examine the plans of the researchers. They ask questions and determine if safeguards are in place. If the research plan is not adequate and safe, it will not receive approval.

All human subjects of legitimate medical research are volunteers. They agree to take part in the study. And these volunteers can help assure their own safety. If they don't feel the doctor has clearly explained the purpose and risks of the experiment, they must insist that they receive the necessary information. This includes the purpose of the experiment, what the subject will be expected to do, how long the study will be going on, what kind of follow-up will be done, and any other questions the subject has.

If all parties do their part—if the researchers develop a good plan and the IRB approves it, and if the volunteer subjects make sure they understand the plan and the risks and are willing to undertake them—then research involving human subjects will remain a safe and invaluable part of medical research.

Benefit to the Patient

Clinical trials not only provide information to researchers; ideally, they help subjects as well. For example, tests of a cancer drug involve subjects who have the disease. So the people who are in the trials have the first chance to try new and advanced treatments. "Although there is always a chance that a new treatment will be disappointing, the researchers involved in a study have reason to believe that it will be as good as, or better than, current treatments,"[4] states a booklet put out by the National Cancer Institute. So the cancer patient who takes part in a clinical trial is helping other cancer patients by testing the treatment, and is potentially helping him- or herself by getting a carefully monitored treatment that may be better than any other available treatment.

This does not mean that there are no risks for human subjects of medical research. Often, unexpected bad side effects will show up when a new treatment is tested. But there are three important things to remember about this: 1) The patient is told about possible risks before the testing begins; he or she decides with open eyes whether or not it is worthwhile to accept those risks. 2) If bad side effects start to occur, the subject can stop the experiment. 3) Perhaps most important, the subjects in a clinical trial are getting much more careful attention and monitoring from their doctors (usually a team of researchers is involved) than they could possibly expect to get in a normal doctor-patient relationship. Therefore, if something bad begins to happen, the patient has the best possible medical care and is surrounded by experts who can help reverse those bad effects.

An unusual example of controversy about human subjects is occurring in the field of AIDS research. Some promising but very experimental drugs are being developed to fight this terrible disease. But some AIDS patients are worried about the length of time it takes to get drugs approved. They fear that they and their friends with HIV or AIDS will be dead before the drugs are approved. They are fighting for the right to take part in human trials even before the drugs have been fully tested in the laboratory and on animal subjects. Some researchers think the AIDS volunteers should be allowed to become research subjects; they clearly understand the risks and they clearly want to participate. But other researchers say it would be unethical to allow these people to test the drugs. They say too much risk is involved. Would it be more ethical to protect the patients by keeping them away from the drugs, or to allow them to possibly receive the benefit of new treatments? The issue has not yet been resolved.

1. Quoted in Sue Berkman, "Volunteering for Medical Research," *Good Housekeeping,* August 1991, p. 165.

2. Quoted in Jennifer Brookes, "Clinical Trials: How They Work, Why We Need Them," *Closing the Gap* (newsletter of the Office of Minority Health, U.S. Department of Health and Human Services), December 1997–January 1998, p. 1.

3. Eugene Passamani, "Clinical Trials—Are They Ethical?" *New England Journal of Medicine,* vol. 324, no. 20, May 30, 1991, p. 1591.

4. "What Are Clinical Trials About?" Office of Cancer Communications, National Cancer Institute, Bethesda, Maryland, 1996, p. 3.

"The regulations for medical research with human subjects must be made much stronger."

Human Research Subjects Need Better Protection

"No expense is spared by this pharmaceutical colossus. The pay is high, the duration of the studies is generally short, and the equipment used is state-of-the art. The catch is that your mental health is not very important to these researchers."[1]

That is what one human "guinea pig" had to say about research with human subjects at a large American drug company. The writer went on to say that a friend had participated in a test to study the effects of a combination of two drugs, an antihistamine and an antidepressant. When the friend's experiment ended, "His mind [was] on the planet Zork. In the following weeks, the man's family and friends went through some terrible grief, and even now, after several months, he is still far from normal and unable to discuss what happened."[2]

The "Rules" Are Not Enough

There are rules for the use of human subjects in medical research, and in theory, this large drug company followed the rules: The subject knew he was going to be involved in research and, in fact, wanted to participate; the research plan was approved by an institutional review board, and the experiment was conducted by appropriate medical personnel. Nevertheless, the subject was not adequately protected. He clearly should have had follow-up care from the doctors involved in the project.

Guidelines Ignored

This may sound like an isolated incident, but it is not. In 1947, the Nuremberg Code, a set of ten guidelines for using human subjects in research, was established. It states that the subjects must know they are going to be a research subject and they must understand the basic plan and the risks involved. If unexpected risks arise, the subject is supposed to be protected. While no country adopted the Nuremberg Code itself as law, many countries, including the United States, created their own regulations based on the Nuremberg Code. These regulations do not stop the endangerment of human subjects, however.

One of the best-known examples is the notorious Tuskegee syphilis study. This study started in 1932, before the world had been shocked by the Nazi atrocities, and before the Nuremberg Code was established. The study took place in Macon, Georgia. The U.S. Public Health Service "intentionally withheld treatment from 399 poor African American men suffering from syphilis. . . . The goal . . . was to observe the long-term effects of syphilis,"[3] states a newsletter from the U.S. Department of Health and Human Services. Syphilis is a venereal disease that, if left untreated, can cause dementia or a variety of physical ailments. It is also a disease that can be successfully treated with penicillin, which was not in wide use for this illness at the time the Tuskegee study started, but which became a standard treatment by the 1940s.

The first scandalous part of this study is that the researchers did not tell the men they were participating in a research project. The progress of their disease was simply studied by the researchers and not treated in any way. The second scandalous part is that the study continued until 1972, long after the Nuremberg Code and later guidelines were developed. Even if the researchers could have claimed that they didn't know any better in 1932 (is it possible that the researchers thought the good they could achieve through their study was worth the lives of 399 men?), they certainly couldn't make that claim in 1950, 1960, or 1970. The study was only stopped because a former Public Health Service employee leaked information about it to the press and public outcry shut it down.

More than three-fourths of the men involved in this study died from complications of syphilis, and most of those who survived became blind and crippled, states Jennifer Brooks in a U.S. Department of Health and Human Services newsletter. Wendy K. Mariner writes that the Tuskegee researchers "became more concerned with the scientific question than with the lives of their research subjects."[4] Researchers gain not only knowledge but sometimes fame and money for their work. The private companies that conduct most of the research gain billions of dollars if a useful drug is developed. They often put a great deal of pressure on their scientists to achieve results regardless of the human cost. The rewards for successful research can sometimes blind corporations and researchers to the human lives they hold in their hands.

"What happened at Tuskegee was terrible," states Dorothy Cirelli of the National Institutes of Health. "But since then, we have put safeguards in place to prevent this from happening again."[5]

It Can Happen Today

Strong words—but say them to the minority women in Africa that an American drug company wants to use as guinea pigs. The drug AZT has shown promise in controlling AIDS in some patients. Now researchers want to discover if giving AZT to pregnant women who have AIDS will prevent their infants from getting the disease. Since certain parts of Africa have very high incidences of AIDS, AZT's manufacturer wants to test the drug there. AZT would be given to one group of HIV-infected pregnant women and not given to a "control" group. (A control group is a "normal" group of people. In the case of drug research, they are usually people who are not given the drug being studied. Their mind or body's reactions to a disease or situation are compared with the reactions of the group that does receive the drug.) The African women would not know if they were getting the drug.

The company's arguments for doing this include 1) that the test would provide information on a drug that holds promise for helping millions of people; 2) that if the drug works as expected, those who receive it will receive direct benefit; and 3) that the people who don't get the drug will be no worse off than they were before. Does this sound like ethical treatment, or does it sound like a repeat of Tuskegee?

Conclusion

These are only three examples of how very unsafe the life of a human guinea pig is. The regulations for medical research with human subjects must be made much stronger, and failure to follow them should lead to a severe penalty. It is not humane to develop products to help one group of people at the expense of the health, sanity, or life of another group.

1. "Research Unit Report Cards," *Guinea Pig Zero: A Journal for Human Pharmaceutical Research Subjects*, No. 2 (1997).

2. "Research Unit Report Cards," *Guinea Pig Zero: A Journal for Human Pharmaceutical Research Subjects*, No. 2 (1997).

3. Jennifer Brookes, "Minority Participation in Clinical Trials," *Closing the Gap* (newsletter of the Office of Minority Health, U.S. Department of Health and Human Services), December 1997–January 1998, p. 3.

4. Wendy K. Mariner, "Public Confidence in Public Health Research Ethics," *Public Health Reports*, January/February 1997, p. 34.

5. Quoted in Brooks, "Minority Participation in Clinical Trials," p. 3.

CHAPTER 2

Organ Transplants

"Adding open commerce to the organ donation process could dramatically increase the number of organs available."

Buying and Selling Organs Is Ethical

Consider the following disturbing statistics:

- "Every year, for each of the 5,500 families that says yes to organ harvesters, another family says no."[1]

- "Many more organs are buried each year than the number of patients needing them. The sad fact is that only 15–25 percent of . . . organs that could be donated are recovered."[2]

- "In the United States alone more than 50,000 people needed a human organ in 1993. More than 2,885 people died before receiving one."[3]

- Of the people who donate organs, "the average [in 1993] was about 3.5 organs per donor,"[4] so an additional 825 donors potentially could have saved the lives of that 2,885 who died.

Insufficient Motivation

Thousands of lives could be saved each year if only organs were available. One person who dies has the potential to provide a heart, two kidneys, a liver, two lungs, two corneas, and a host of other organs to those who require them. There is no question that enough people die to provide the desperately needed organs, but not a great enough percentage of those who die and their families agree to organ donation. As Andy H. Barnett and his cowriters say, "Our current public policy has failed miserably to address the organ shortage."[6] A major reason for this failure is that people are not motivated enough to donate.

In the first place, the need for donation is not publicized enough, but even if it were, the only motivation offered for donation is altruism—that is, the dying patient or his or her family agree to give the organs out of an unselfish wish to put another's welfare first. While this is indeed a noble reason, it is not strong enough for many people to overcome revulsion (reluctance for themselves or a loved one to be carved up into pieces), grief (many people are too stricken with grief and the need to take care of things like medical bills and burial details to add one more concern to their mental load), and apathy (they haven't been made to care enough about what the gift of organs can do).

If everyone agreed to be an organ donor, there would be no shortage of organs for transplant. The reasons people refuse to donate are complex.

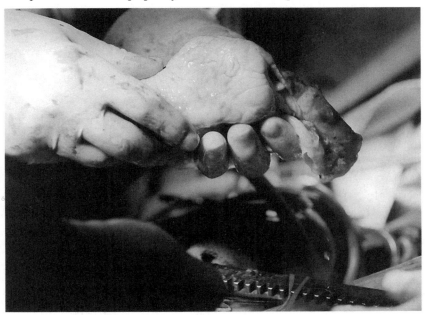

The United States is a free-market society. Supply and demand determines a commodity's value, and almost everything can be bought or sold. It is clear that if organs were allowed to become part of the free-market process, the organ shortage would be solved, or at least decreased. Once a monetary value is placed on organs, people would become more aware of the opportunity to do good, and they would gain some compensation for themselves or their heirs as well.

Some say this view is crass—that organ donation should remain a donation and not become a business deal. But that is not realistic. Few people do things purely for the good of others. Doctors charge for their services and so do teachers; ministers charge for the use of the church for wedding ceremonies and baptisms, and undertakers charge for funerals; caretakers charge for baby-sitting and garage owners charge for changing oil. The wheels of commerce make the engine of America run smoothly. Adding open commerce to the organ donation process could dramatically increase the number of organs available. Additionally, a financially motivated donation program would ultimately improve the quality of organs available (presently, doctors often implant imperfect organs because of the scarcity), and it would bring down the price of transplants. As Merrill Matthews Jr. states, "In virtually every sector of the economy where price and competition play a role, quality increases and cost decreases."[7]

Commercialism Is Already a Factor

Another consideration is that the donor market is already financially based to a great extent. Organ transplantation is an extremely costly process. In 1988 it cost from $16,000 to $21,000 simply for obtaining the organ, and many thousands more for the surgical transplant procedure, follow-up medical care, and antirejection and other drugs the transplant patient often must continue to take for the rest of his or her life. Many insurance policies do not cover these costs in full— some exclude transplant coverage entirely. So people who are uninsured or underinsured are often not even allowed onto a transplantation waiting list because of their lack of ability to pay.

Occasional news stories make it clear that celebrities and the rich and powerful are more likely to receive an organ than the ordinary person. In 1996, for example, many people were scandalized when baseball legend Mickey Mantle received a liver transplant two days after he discovered he needed one, while many people wait for months and even years before they get an organ.

The organ market is alive and well in many developing countries, but even in the United States, there is evidence that an underground market for organs has developed. Matthews states that "the shortage of organs is so chronic that international organized crime has become involved."[8] Many examples, from liquor in the 1920s and 1930s to illegal drugs today, show that where there is prohibition, there is likely to be a black market.

By allowing the opportunity to legally buy and sell organs, the commercial process would be brought into the open and the organ pool would be increased and upgraded in quality. Andy H. Barnett writes that legalizing organ purchase and sale "would vastly increase the number of organs made available for transplantation, thereby saving numerous lives. Both organ recipients and organ donors (or suppliers) would benefit from such free-market exchange."[9]

Marketing Systems

There are many ways this could be done. Matthews suggests four: One method would simply repeal the laws against organ selling and allow people to buy and sell as they wish.

Another method would develop a futures market in organs. Futures markets are common in agriculture. People buy grain today that hasn't even been planted yet. They hope that when the grain is grown and harvested, it will be worth more than they paid. Something similar could be done with organs:

People could sell the future right to their heart, for example, and get the money now. When they die, the buyer would own the heart. Buyers could then sell it to someone who needs it. As with grain, the buyer would be gambling that the organ would be worth more later than he or she paid today.

A third method would allow organs to be considered part of a person's estate. Arrangements for this would have to be made ahead of time because of the short viability of harvested organs; most have to be transplanted within a matter of hours or days. So the donor would arrange that after his or her death, an organ buyer would pay the estate the going rate.

A fourth method would establish a donor pool similar to many barter or exchange systems. All members would agree to donate their organs after death, but only people who belong to the pool—who have agreed to donate their organs—would be eligible to receive any organs from the pool.

All of these methods would offer some benefits to both rich and poor. To belong to an organ pool, for example, you would not have to be rich and you would be assured of having a replacement organ when you need one. This is a much better guarantee than anyone has today, and it would be a much stronger motivation to donate organs than simply doing it out of the goodness of your heart. The other three systems all offer monetary gain, another powerful motivator.

Little Risk of Corruption

Some people fear that if systems like those described above were put into place, corruption would occur: Poor people would be forced to sell their "spare" kidney to the highest bidder; doctors who knew a person was a donor would stop treatment early and allow the patient to die; criminals would kill people for their organs or make the black market in organs even bigger than it is today. None of these things is likely to happen, however. A free market with stronger motivations for people to give their organs would soon provide enough organs to fill all needs. With plenty of available organs, prices would drop, and no one would have an incentive to do the bad things some people fear.

It is clear that something must be done to end the organ shortage. The free-market system would seem to be the most practical, efficient, and beneficial to all members of society.

1. Stephen Baker, "Who Gets a Liver—and Who Doesn't?" *Business Week*, December 9, 1996, p. 153.

2. Quoted in Tamara L. Roleff, ed., *Biomedical Ethics*. San Diego: Greenhaven Press, 1998, p. 54.

3. Merrill Matthews Jr., "Have a Heart, But Pay for It," *Insight on the News*, January 9, 1995, p. 18.

4. Matthews, "Have a Heart, But Pay for It," p. 18.

5. Jeanne Marie Laskas, "Angel of the Heart Ward," *Good Housekeeping*, November 1997, p. 125.

6. Quoted in Roleff, *Biomedical Ethics*, p. 53.

7. Matthews, "Have a Heart, But Pay for It," p. 20.

8. Matthews, "Have a Heart, But Pay for It," p. 18.

9. Quoted in Roleff, *Biomedical Ethics*, p. 55.

"Buying and selling organs . . . devalues human beings
and turns them into commodities or products."

Buying and Selling Organs Is Unethical

In India, some impoverished people sell a kidney or a cornea in order to provide their family with basic needs. In China, officials sell the organs of executed prisoners. In Missouri, the legislature proposed a bill that would commute death-row inmates' sentences to life imprisonment in exchange for giving up a healthy organ for transplantation. Proposals have been made to have a "futures market" in organs; that is, a person would accept compensation now for agreeing to donate an organ when he or she dies.

What's wrong with these situations? As newspaper columnist Ellen Goodman points out, "We do let people sell blood, hair, sperm. We've paid surrogate mothers and egg donors." Yet, she adds, "We have been quite properly queasy about the free-market approach to the human body. There are some things that aren't and shouldn't be for sale—among them an 'extra' cornea or 'spare' kidney."[1]

Unhealthy Greed

The basis of Goodman's view is found in the old saying "Money is the root of all evil." While that may be overgeneralizing a bit, it is true that all too often where money is concerned, greed overwhelms all other considerations. All too often, those who stand to gain the most will place more value on the end (money or a needed organ) than on the means (the mutilation or death of another human being).

In the case of the Chinese prisoners, for example, Goodman says that "it's even been reported that prisoners with prime organs and ready customers get bumped to the front of the execution line."[2] And a suspicious number of Chinese prisoners is executed each year—more than four thousand in 1997, many of them for minor crimes. If the Chinese government—or worse yet, prison administrators or guards—gets money from the sale of prisoners' organs, what's to stop it from executing even more people for even less serious crimes?

The United States presently has laws against buying and selling organs. If those laws were changed, the greed of some very bad people could become even stronger. British writer Alasdair Palmer says, "Making it acceptable for hospitals to purchase organs would immediately encourage the thugs already in the market to step up their work-rate. Criminal gangs are already

known to have kidnapped children for their organs in Russia and South America."[3] What's to prevent them from conducting the same kind of horrifying operations here?

Devaluing Human Life

Another thing that's wrong with buying and selling organs is that it devalues human beings and turns them into commodities or products. The value of the individual person might be forgotten if something else of high value can be gained. Commentator Malcolm Muggeridge writes, "To me these [organ sales] have something very creepy and unpleasant about them. . . . The cadaver has come to have a market value, leaving no place for requiems, prayers, or mourning with kidneys, hearts, eyeballs, and other such items up for sale."[4]

Think about the temptation: If you had a relative whose death was inevitable, would you be enticed to stop his or her treatment early if you knew you would get money for any organs harvested? If you wouldn't go that far, would you breathe a sigh of relief when the patient finally died and you could pay some bills or take a dreamed-of trip? That kind of temptation can't help but make people forget, at least a little, that the dying patient is a human being.

It's unfortunate that the value of the individual is even more likely to be forgotten at a corporate or organizational level. Right now, some families complain that when they have a dying loved one, hospital personnel pester them to agree to donate the person's organs. That leads to the unfortunate fear that the hospital might not do everything it can to save the loved one's life. After all, if the hospital can acquire organs through the patient's death, it will be gaining something of great value for no cost. What will make medical personnel remember that the patient is a real human being, loved and treasured by family and friends?

How to Get More Organs

Many people suggest that the only way to solve the organ shortage is to allow organs to be bought and sold, but that's not true.

There are other ways. The first thing that needs to be done is to give the cause of organ donation much more publicity and make every person aware of the possibility of donation. This can be done with a strong advertising campaign. Just like companies that sell gasoline, cigarettes, and bungee jumping, the medical community can sell the idea of organ donation. Stephen Baker, a business writer, reports a terrific idea that deserves a try: In 1996, "Michael Jordan lent his image to a national campaign, and now, organ-procurement organizations are circulating 5 million donor cards embossed with the basketball idol's picture."[5] If a superstar's endorsement can sell $150 sneakers, why not the organ donation program?

Bioethicist Arthur Caplan suggests a variation of this plan. Instead of attempting to make organ donation look "cool," we should spend time reeducating people to view organ donation not as a gift, but as a duty.

Another approach would be to change the present policy of informed consent. Informed consent in this context means that before a person's organs are harvested, he or she has to explicitly indicate that the organs are to be donated. People who want to donate must carry an organ donor card, make their wishes known to their physician, or sign consent papers at the hospital saying that they want to donate their organs. Some countries have changed the policy in one of two ways. Linda C. Fentiman writes that "several European countries, as well as Israel, New Zealand, Singapore, and Tunisia have already instituted a system of presumed consent."[6] Presumed consent means that if people don't explicitly make known that they *don't* want their organs donated, it will be presumed that it's OK to harvest them. That way many organs can be obtained from people who simply didn't get around to filling out a donor card or telling people their intentions.

The second proposed alternative to informed consent is to have the government take a more active role in acquiring people's consent. All driver's licenses, for example, would have a check-off option that people must fill in. They would have to state whether or not they wanted their organs donated. That system would allow for informed consent and would avoid the problems caused by people who procrastinate or who haven't given any thought to organ donation.

Artificial Organs

A third approach to ending or reducing the organ shortage would be to put more money into developing artificial organs or to make more use of animal organs that can replace human ones. World Heart Corporation's aim is "to replace organ transplants with compact, self-sufficient artificial hearts or partial hearts . . . that could stay inside patients for life."[7] At present, artificial hearts are used as a temporary measure, to tide a patient over until a human heart is available. If World Heart and its competitors can successfully develop a permanent artificial heart, that particular organ shortage will be ended.

It's clear that something must be done to alleviate the organ shortage, but buying and selling human organs is not the answer. It's time to look for alternatives that are efficient and ethical.

1. Ellen Goodman, "The Body as Commodity," Washington Post Writers Group, March 10, 1998.

2. Goodman, "The Body as Commodity."

3. Quoted in Tamara L. Roleff, ed., *Biomedical Ethics*. San Diego: Greenhaven Press, 1998, p. 67.

4. Quoted in Terry O'Neill, ed., *Biomedical Ethics*. San Diego: Greenhaven Press, 1994, p. 70.

5. Stephen Baker, "Who Gets a Liver—and Who Doesn't?" *Business Week*, December 9, 1996, p. 153.

6. Quoted in Tamara L. Roleff, ed., *Biomedical Ethics*. San Diego: Greenhaven Press, 1998, p. 76.

7. Ian Austen, "Stock Ticker," *Canadian Business*, September 26, 1997, p. 114.

CHAPTER 3

Genetic Technology

"Genetic testing can . . . give people the knowledge needed to prevent diseases to which they are genetically predisposed."

Genetic Testing Is Beneficial

"Within 30 years, researchers expect to be able to produce a [complete] genetic 'fingerprint' of an individual's potential future health that will enable doctors to wage pre-emptive battle,"[1] states *Time* magazine. This means that with genetic tests, doctors will be able to tell what diseases each patient is likely to get. The doctor can then provide treatments or recommend changes in lifestyle that will prevent or reduce the effects of those diseases.

Even today, scientific advances have made it possible for people to be tested for genetic connections to certain diseases. Sometimes this knowledge can lead to prevention of the disease. For example, "Ann" was diagnosed with a genetic disease of the colon that leads to cancer. She had two young daughters at the time. When her daughters were ten and twelve, she had them genetically tested and found that they too carried the gene linked to that condition. When they were a little older, doctors removed the girls' colons, "greatly reducing their cancer risk,"[2] writes Lyric Wallwork Winik in *Parade* magazine. This is called a prophylactic, or preventive, operation. This kind of surgery is extreme, but for those who are at high risk, many think it is a better alternative than risking death from painful, lingering cancer.

Genetic testing can also simplify diagnosis of potential health problems. Doctors encourage people to undergo regular physical examinations that include tests for certain diseases. For example, women are urged to have a pap smear each year. An abnormal pap smear result can mean that the woman has a disease of her reproductive organs and may have to go through a long series of additional tests to try to discover what's causing the abnormality. Now that genetic testing is available, doctors can quickly determine whether the woman carries the genes related to certain diseases, thereby eliminating the need for lengthy tests.

David Stipp writes in *Fortune* magazine about a test for one type of genetic disease that strikes many women: "The results were impressive. Genotyping flagged probable incipient [early] cancers the smears missed, and ruled out cancer in many patients who traditionally undergo costly follow-ups."[3]

Stipp also notes that "a doctor can use one of the new tests to find out whether a seemingly routine infection involves dangerous bacteria with genes conferring resistance to the usual antibiotics."[4] If this is the case, the doctor will know to try a different method of treatment to combat the disease.

Preparing for the Future

Genetic testing can also help people prepare for the future. Many diseases are inherited genetically. Certain families carry a gene that increases their likelihood of getting cancer; others carry a gene for cystic fibrosis (a disease that causes lung and digestive system deterioration), sickle-cell anemia (a blood disease in which malformed blood cells are unable to carry the proper amount of oxygen to the body's tissues, causing tiredness, jaundice [a liver disease], and shortness of breath), or Tay-Sachs (a fatal disease of the nervous system). People who have one of these diseases in their families may decide to have genetic testing done to help them decide whether or not to have children.

Genetic testing can also give people the knowledge needed to prevent diseases to which they are genetically predisposed.

Genetic testing may help curb birth complications by allowing doctors to know exactly what medical problems an unborn infant may encounter. Here, Donna and Mike Chandler sit with their two children, Brian and Carrie. Both children have been diagnosed with the genetic disease cystic fibrosis.

One of the most common American killers is cancer. As with many diseases, the genetic link to cancer is only one of the factors involved. The *Tufts University Health & Nutrition Letter* states, "With cancer . . . finding an abnormal gene means you are one 'hit' closer than a person without the gene to contracting the cancer . . . not that you will automatically develop a malignant tumor."[5] By changing lifestyle (diet and exercise, smoking and drinking habits, for example), a person with a cancer gene might be able to prevent or delay cancer.

Psychological Effects

Some genetic diseases are fatal. Dr. Tim Wolter worries that people who discover they have the gene for one of these diseases will suffer despair, knowing there is no cure. Someday, he says, scientists may be able to counteract "bad" genes with gene therapy, but medical science is not advanced enough yet.

He writes that

> our ability to call forth this wonderful, terrible infor-
> mation is in its infancy. As the human genome is
> steadily mapped out in the decade to come, we will
> see a Pandora's box of human genetics slowly yawn
> open. Hope, in the form of true "gene therapy" will
> probably be the last thing out of the box, another
> generation in coming, and in the interim, how much
> of what we learn will be things we would be happier
> not knowing?[6]

Wolter suggests that no good can come from knowing how
you are going to die, but some people believe that even this
kind of knowledge is helpful. Darla Brockus is a young mother whose family carries the gene for ataxia, an incurable disease in which the brain cells that control movement gradually
waste away. Darla told *Glamour* magazine, "It's good to be
able to prepare your family both financially and emotionally."[7]

If a disease runs in a family, members can be tested to find
out whether they are likely to get the disease. If the test is negative, they can breathe a sigh of relief and go on with their life.
If the test is positive, they know they now have time to prepare for the disease, or try to avoid it. With proper counseling, people can learn to deal with even the most disturbing
outcome of a genetic test.

The Discrimination Factor

A frequent criticism of genetic testing is that it can lead to discrimination in the workplace and by insurance companies.
Once a person is known to have a genetic predisposition
toward cancer or another disease that involves costly treatment, health insurance companies may refuse to insure that
person. An employer may not want to hire that person.

Kathleen Kennedy Townsend says the concern about discrimination is misplaced. As more is learned about genes and
disease, it becomes clear that almost everyone has a genetic

inheritance relating to some disease. Already scientists have discovered particular diseases related to almost every ethnic group. "Before long," she writes, "scientists will uncover the genetic roots to more and more diseases, and it will be more possible than ever—for ourselves, our doctors, and our insurance companies—to predict who will come down with what illness. . . . Before long we will *all* be uninsurable."[8]

Obviously, if they have no one to insure, insurance companies will go out of business. Since they don't want to do that, discrimination will no longer be an issue. Or better yet, according to Townsend's view, the United States will finally institute a national health care plan that will cover medical costs for every citizen, no matter what their medical history or their genetic make-up. England, Canada, Sweden, and many other countries already have such plans in effect.

The bottom line on genetic testing is that it's a good thing. With it doctors and their patients can learn how to make people healthier, even if they have genes that suggest they should be otherwise.

1. Jill Smolowe, "Seeing the Future," *Time*, Special Issue: Heroes of Medicine, Fall 1997, p. 38.

2. Lyric Wallwork Winik, "When You Should Consider a Genetic Test," *Parade*, April 19, 1998, p. 8.

3. David Stipp, "Gene Testing Starts to Pay Off: Medical Miracles," *Fortune*, August 4, 1997, p. 25.

4. Stipp, "Gene Testing Starts to Pay Off," p. 25.

5. "When Genetic Testing Might Be Appropriate: The Role of the Genetic Counselor," *Tufts University Health & Nutrition Letter*, March 1998, p. 8.

6. Tim Wolter, "There Are Simply Some Things We Should Not Know," *American Medical News*, April 7, 1997, p. 19.

7. Quoted in Tamara L. Roleff, ed., *Biomedical Ethics*. San Diego: Greenhaven Press, 1998, p. 203.

8. Kathleen Kennedy Townsend, "The Double-Edged Helix: Advances in Genetic Testing Reveal Yet Another Reason We Need National Health Insurance," *Washington Monthly*, November 1997, p. 36.

"While genetic testing clearly has some benefits, the potential harms are far worse."

Genetic Testing Is Harmful

In 1996 National Public Radio reported the case of a young man in his early twenties whose family had a history of a fatal genetic disease. Since he knew he was likely to die within a few years, he obtained several credit cards and ran them up to their limits. He participated in meaningless sexual encounters (why try to develop a relationship, he thought, when neither of us will be able to enjoy it for long?). Although he was intelligent, he did not go to college or otherwise prepare for a career. Then, encouraged by his family doctor, he underwent genetic testing and was stunned to discover that he did not carry the particular gene that caused the disease; barring accident, he was going to live a normal life. Now he was faced with the overwhelming task of putting his woefully messed-up life back into shape. The prospect almost drove him to suicide.

Psychological Consequences

Presumably this young man's case is uncommon, but it does point up one of the dangers of genetic testing: the psychological consequences. Today, with genetic testing, it is possible to discover whether you have a gene that indicates you will likely develop certain forms of cancer, the degenerative disease called Huntington's, Alzheimer's, and several other frightening diseases. But is this something people should know? The positive aspect is that with some diseases, knowing ahead of time can lead to treatment or preventative measures. For example, if you have a gene related to breast cancer, by changing eating and exercise habits and increasing regular medical checkups you can reduce your chances of getting the cancer, or increase your chances of finding it early enough to treat it.

But for every disease like breast cancer, there are others for which there is no successful treatment at this time. A thirty-seven-year-old woman named Ruth was happily married and had two young children when she found out that her family carried the gene for Huntington's disease. The symptoms of Huntington's do not usually appear until middle age or later, but once they begin the victim suffers quick degeneration of both mental and physical faculties. Ruth knew that if she came down with the disease, her family would have to care for her as she grew progressively more sick, weak, helpless, and mentally deranged. She couldn't stand the thought. "I believe that if you know you're at risk but don't know if you have the gene, you'll live your life like you have the disease," she said. She decided to have the genetic test for Huntington's, and if it turned out that she had the gene, she would "find a good housekeeper for her husband and sons, then disappear," reports Jill Smolowe. "I wanted to spare my family,"[1] Ruth told the reporter.

Ruth was fortunate. The test showed she did not carry the lethal gene. One would think she could now live happily ever after, but that was not the case. Smolowe reports that "within a year of testing negative, [Ruth] separated from her husband. 'I didn't know what I wanted anymore. A lot of decisions I made didn't make sense. I just wanted to be free.'"[2]

Ruth's reaction may be typical of those who fear they have a genetic death sentence hanging over their head. The burden is not necessarily lifted with a negative test result. Many times people get tested because a family member has the feared disease. When they find out they don't have the gene, they feel guilty for being spared when a loved one has to suffer. And for those whose results are positive—well, can you imagine what it would feel like to know that you are likely to get an incurable disease in the foreseeable future?

Practical Consequences

Another major problem with genetic testing is the impact it can have on a person's career and insurance coverage. "Insurance companies have always looked for better ways to weed out those who may one day fall ill, and, consequently, need expensive treatment,"[3] writes Kathleen Kennedy Townsend. And positive results from genetic testing can give them the ammunition they need.

Insurance files are filled with cases of people whose costly medical care was not covered because of pre-existing conditions (health conditions that are either known or can be shown to have existed before the insurance took effect; a person with a history of back problems, for example, might not be covered for medical treatment for the back if he or she got a new insurance policy). Few conditions fit the "pre-existing" label better than genetically caused diseases, since genes are in place from the moment of conception.

Kathleen Kennedy Townsend gives the example of a postal worker who had held the same job for twenty years with no problems. When he lost his vision, his insurance company refused to cover his medical bills because his problem was caused by a genetic disease he didn't even know he had.

There are laws in place that are supposed to protect people from insurance discrimination based on genetic test results, but insurance companies can find ways to get around them. The medical director of a large Canadian insurance company says that if a woman has a family history of breast cancer, his company would not be able to discriminate against her because of that. However, "I'll scrutinize her record extra carefully. I'll rate her for hypertension [high blood pressure].

I'll hope there is something else I can find in the record to rate her on. . . . I won't tell her I rated her [as a] higher [medical risk] than someone else with the same hypertension."[4]

Insurance companies can find ways to refuse coverage or charge higher premiums to those with problems discovered through a genetic test. Employers can also discriminate on the basis of genetic information. If they have the information ahead of time, why would an employer hire someone they know is going to be sick a lot and cost the company money in lost time and medical benefits? If they discover the problem during employment, they might practice other forms of discrimination.

One notorious case happened at Lawrence Berkeley Laboratory in Berkeley, California. At Lawrence Berkeley, "Management tested African-American workers for sickle-cell anemia and the genetic trait for the disease for more than a decade—without workers' consent. . . . All along, workers thought they were giving urine and blood samples for cholesterol screening."[5] (African Americans are almost two hundred times more likely to carry the gene for sickle-cell anemia than are whites.) Lawrence Berkeley used these secret tests to find out which black employees carried the gene, and then they denied promotions and otherwise discriminated against these employees.

Privacy Invasion

The frightening thing about discrimination based on genetic testing is that the results are so easy for insurance companies and employers to obtain. Most companies keep their employee records on computer databases. Viewing information in a database is not difficult for those who know how. Also, if a person has a genetic test done and the doctor submits the cost of the test to the insurance company for payment, the insurance company now has that information as well. Many genetic test results are negative and many positive results do not mean the person will ever develop symptoms of the disease,

but that doesn't matter where discrimination is concerned. If you've had the test, you are vulnerable to losing health care coverage, to paying increased rates, to not getting the job you want, or to suffering other forms of discrimination.

If you know that your family has a tendency to a particular kind of disease and you think you should be tested, Wendy McGoodwin, director of the Council for Responsible Genetics, recommends that you do these three things to protect your privacy:

1) Pay for the test yourself.

2) Ask your doctor to keep your results in a high-security file and/or not to put them in your medical record.

3) Purchase any insurance policies *before* undergoing genetic testing.[6]

While genetic testing clearly has some benefits, the potential harms are far worse. From the psychological impact to the practical effects, the negative side effects should make one stop and think very hard before submitting to a genetic test.

1. Quoted in Jill Smolowe, "Seeing the Future," *Time*, Special Issue: Heroes of Medicine, Fall 1997, p. 40.

2. Quoted in Smolowe, "Seeing the Future," p 39.

3. Kathleen Kennedy Townsend, "The Double-Edged Helix: Advances in Genetic Testing Reveal Yet Another Reason We Need National Health Insurance," *Washington Monthly*, November 1997, p. 36.

4. Quoted in Townsend, "The Double-Edged Helix," p. 37.

5. Samuel Greengard, "Genetic Testing: Should You Be Afraid? It's No Joke," *Workforce*, July 1997, p. 40.

6. Quoted in Lyric Wallwork Winik, "When You Should Consider a Genetic Test," *Parade*, April 19, 1998, p. 6.

"By using gene therapy on . . . 'bad' genes, [scientists] can prevent many fatal and debilitating illnesses."

Gene Therapy Can Eliminate Disease

In 1990, waves of public sympathy went out to a little boy named David when his story was told in a national magazine. David came to be known as the "bubble boy" because of the plastic room, or "bubble," in which he lived. The transparent room was closed off to the rest of the world. David's food, clothing, and other needs were carefully sterilized and passed to him through air locks in the bubble's walls. David had a rare genetic disease that made him unusually sensitive to every kind of germ. If he came in contact with one, he could become very sick and die. David had lived in the bubble for nine years. David's disease was called ADA deficiency, because a gene caused a deficiency, or lack, of an enzyme that helps the immune system fight off disease.

Scientists did not want other children to have to live like David. In the early 1980s they had already begun experimenting, trying to find some way to compensate for the harmful gene. They managed to isolate a normal, nondeficient gene. In the laboratory, they put copies of this gene into the cells of an ADA-deficient patient. They found that with this combination, the ADA patient's cells could manufacture enough of the enzyme to fight off infection.

Once they were successful in the lab, the scientists tried

injecting "corrected" cells into the bloodstream of two little girls, four and nine years old, who had ADA deficiency. After a year of treatments every month or so, the children had developed improved immunity. Science writer Eric S. Grace reports that the youngest girl "was able to attend school, swim, dance, and ice-skate with her family and friends with no more risk of catching infections than they had."[1] The other child, too, was able to lead a relatively normal life. Since this treatment has worked so well on these two girls, many people hope that now children like David will no longer have to be isolated from the rest of the world.

Gene Therapy

These children benefited from gene therapy, the practice of changing, killing, or replacing genes that cause disease. It is a relatively new science, made possible by the Human Genome

Project, a fifteen-year international effort to identify and map the entire human genome, a group of sixty thousand to eighty thousand genes.

Our genes determine all of our physical characteristics and some of our psychological characteristics as well. As scientists have learned more about genes, they have found that a tremendous number of diseases, or susceptibility to them, are caused by genes. A few examples are arthritis, asthma, numerous cancers, diabetes, high blood pressure, schizophrenia, and depres-

Scientists believe that mapping the human genome can lead to gene therapy, the ability to replace "bad" genes with "good" genes.

sion. Most of these diseases are caused by a specific gene out of the thousands the body's cells carry. Genetic scientists are working hard to find the particular gene that causes each of these diseases and many more. They believe that by using gene therapy on the "bad" genes, they can prevent many fatal and debilitating illnesses, and they can stop or cure others.

Suicide Genes

Altering disease-causing genes, as was done for the children with ADA, is one approach scientists are using. Another is using "suicide genes." This has been successfully used on patients with glioblastoma, a fast-growing brain tumor. Reporter Jeff Goldberg writes of a glioblastoma patient named Betty Perr. Doctors injected

> mouse skin cells carrying a genetically altered mouse leukemia virus into Perr's brain. The mouse virus contains a gene from the herpes simplex virus that causes cold sores. . . . [Other parts of the mouse cells' DNA have been removed] to cripple the virus, so that it can infect but not reproduce in human cells. In particular, the cells can infect only multiplying cells, which means that the only brain cells infected will be tumor cells, because normal brain cells do not divide. Once infected by the virus, the tumor cells will produce [a chemical] making them vulnerable to [an] antiviral drug.[2]

The virus that was injected into Perr's brain is called a suicide virus because it cannot reproduce and it cannot attack healthy brain cells. It goes into the brain and attacks the multiplying tumor cells at the cost of its own life—it can be killed by a drug similar to that used to get rid of cold sores. Betty Perr, one of the first to have this treatment, did not survive long. But other patients this technique has been used on have survived at a high percentage, and doctors are certain that with more study this treatment will become even more successful.

Other Treatments

For patients with cancer, often the best treatment is chemotherapy or radiotherapy (using high doses of tumor-killing chemicals or radiation). Although these treatments are aimed at the cancerous cells, they also affect surrounding healthy cells and cause many side effects, including severe nausea, hair loss, exhaustion, and reduced immunity to germs and viruses. Sometimes the side effects are so bad they send the patient into deep depression or are the cause of the patient's becoming ill from something besides cancer.

Scientists studying cancer have discovered a promising gene therapy that may eliminate these side effects. Inside cancer cells they found a gene they call MDR1. This gene makes cells resistant to radiation and chemotherapy. In cancer cells, this is a bad thing, because the gene makes the cancer less responsive to the radiation and chemotherapy. However, researchers found a way to take some of this gene out of the cancer and return it to the patient's body in a way that makes it join healthy cells. Now it's the healthy cells that have become resistant to chemical and radiation therapies, thus allowing doctors to use higher doses and be more assured of killing the cancer without harming healthy cells or causing the patient to become desperately ill from the treatment.

Still other research promises that with gene therapy, doctors may be able to "disrupt a tumor's ability to generate new blood vessels,"[3] according to writer Susan Jenks. In this treatment the therapeutic genes will act as a "tourniquet," squeezing off a tumor's blood supply.

Scientists are also experimenting with genes that will allow hearts to "grow their own bypasses," writes reporter Daniel Q. Haney. Many patients with heart disease need bypass surgery, in which doctors sever, or cut apart, blood vessels, reconnecting healthy parts and bypassing the clogged or weakened parts. Sometimes they use artificial veins or balloonlike devices to expand the vessels. But doctors at St. Elizabeth's Medical Center in Boston have injected extra genes into the heart "that will trigger it to sprout new blood vessels within two to three weeks." The new vessels will "carry blood around the blockages,"[4] Haney reports. Thus the patients will not need the more extreme bypass surgery.

Gene Therapy and Alcoholism

It is not only obvious physical ailments that gene therapy can cure. Researchers in San Francisco believe that someday soon gene therapy may be used to cure alcoholism. University of California scientists have been studying the effects of alcohol on fruit flies. (Yes, these tiny little insects are frequently used for study of human problems. Their biological functions are similar in many ways to humans', and because their lives are so brief, scientists can see the effects of gene therapy—and other treatments—over many generations in a short time.)

According to a report in the *Los Angeles Times*, the researchers have found that the fruit flies most strongly affected by alcohol have a mutated (changed) gene. The normal form of the gene produces a chemical called cAMP. The mutated gene does not produce as much of this chemical. By giving the flies a drug that increases cAMP production, alcohol's effect is weakened. The researchers believe the knowledge they've discovered in this experiment will help them end human alcoholism.

A Promising Future

There is no question that gene therapy is well on its way to ending human disease. At present, scientists know of around four thousand diseases that are caused by genes. By learning how to identify the correct genes, and then to alter, add to, or kill the offending ones, science will finally bring us to a state where cancer, lung disease, and other illnesses will no longer be the leading causes of death.

1. Eric S. Grace, "Better Health Through Gene Therapy," *Futurist*, January/February 1998, p. 40.

2. Jeff Goldberg, "A Head Full of Hope," *Discover*, April 1998, p. 70.

3. Susan Jenks, "Gene Therapy: A New Role in Disrupting Tumor's Blood Supply?" *Journal of the National Cancer Institute*, February 18, 1998, p. 270.

4. Daniel Q. Haney, "Need a Bypass? Someday You Can Grow Your Own," Associated Press, November 10, 1997.

"Conventional methods will still be easier, more reliable, and cheaper than trying to eliminate and cure disease with gene therapy."

Gene Therapy Won't End Disease

Gene therapy offers much promise in ending and curing certain types of diseases, but to say that it will end disease is absolutely wrong. In fact, society may eventually discover that it causes more harm than good.

Not on the Horizon

In the first place, those who champion gene therapy talk as though the cures for terrible diseases like cancer, Huntington's, Alzheimer's, and cystic fibrosis are just over the horizon. They talk as though it will be only a few months or years before science knows how to end these diseases. In reality, it is likely to be decades before any genetic diseases are ended with gene therapy. This science is still in its infancy.

Scientists began their intensive study of human genes about a decade ago. By 1998 they had managed to identify and figure out the purpose of about fifteen thousand genes. But the human body has somewhere between sixty thousand and eighty thousand genes, many of them probably linked to diseases. Scientists aim to have human gene identification completed by about 2005, but that doesn't seem realistic, considering that we are more than halfway to 2005 and much less than halfway finished identifying genes.

Once scientists are able to link a particular gene to a particular disease, they still need to figure out how to deal with that gene to end the disease. Maybe they have to replace it; maybe they have to kill it; maybe they have to add another type of gene to combat the disease. All of the experimenting involved in this type of research takes many years. As science writer Gina Maranto writes, "While a number of genetic ailments might one day be controlled or eliminated by gene therapy, scientists will probably still be laboring well into the next century to refine the technology."[1]

Unreliability

Perhaps a worse problem is that much of the "promising" research that has been done really hasn't accomplished much at all. Gretchen Vogel writes in *Science* magazine that "the technology doesn't work very well. Seven years after the first gene-therapy trial in humans, the technique has yet to produce a definitive [absolute] cure for a single patient." She states that geneticists are "having trouble delivering DNA into target cells and getting transplanted genes to work for more than a few months."[2]

Research is still very limited. Doctors have tried gene therapy on only two patients with ADA, a disorder that prevents the body from fighting disease. While the therapy seems to have worked pretty well on these two people, that's hardly enough of a test to know how it will react on other patients. In the late 1990s, doctors at M.D. Anderson Hospital at the University of Texas, Austin, tried gene therapy on fifty-three hundred patients who had brain cancer. The therapy seemed to work on only about one-third of the patients—two-thirds died. Worse, as the widow of one of the patients said, "They don't know why it didn't work."[3]

All too often, that's the case with gene therapy. Scientists don't really understand what makes it work or not work; they are experimenting. Journalist Helen Thorpe writes that gene therapy is "wildly promising but still far from reliable." She adds:

The public seems to expect doctors to be able to fix chronic medical problems by tinkering with genetic material like a mechanic under the hood of a car, [but] years of research need to be done before gene therapy fulfills its potential. . . . If it can someday be perfected, it will indeed resemble a miracle—it will be an alternative for people who cannot be treated by more conventional means.[4]

Thorpe and other experts are convinced that gene therapy will be the exception, not the rule; that is, it will only be practical to use it on patients who don't respond to other treatment. It will not become commonplace. Antibiotics and other, more conventional methods will still be easier, more reliable, and cheaper than trying to eliminate and cure disease with gene therapy.

A Disease-Free Society?

Even if gene therapy could be made reliable, disease could not be entirely eliminated. John Maddox, editor of the journal *Nature*, writes, "It is an illusion to think that a genetically 'pure' society could ever be created. Many disease-linked genes arise spontaneously in apparently normal families, including Huntington's disease and Fragile X syndrome (which is one of the most common genetic causes of inherited mental defect)."[5] In other words, genes are somewhat unpredictable, and outside influences affect them.

Today we know that a particular gene is linked to breast cancer, but having that gene doesn't mean that a person will get the disease, and not having the gene doesn't mean the person won't get the disease. Other important elements include the person's diet and exercise practices, whether they have unhealthy habits like smoking, factors in the environment (including physical elements like pollution, but also including psychological factors like stress), and plain old luck. Take any two people, give them perfect genes and similar lifestyles, and it would still be the luck of the draw whether either of them developed cancer.

Perfect Genes?

The goal of genetic scientists seems to be to give everyone perfect genes. Once "bad" genes can be recognized, they will be fixed, replaced, or removed. But humans being what they are, this is unlikely to stop at ending disease. Science will move from medical therapy to enhancement therapy, from curing diseases to making people more attractive or smarter. Dr. Sheila M. Rothman of Columbia University says that tampering is part of human nature. "Human beings have sought to enhance their capabilities through their own efforts 'ever since Prometheus stole fire,'" she asserts, adding that in a sense, humans are "'a manmade species.'"[6]

Once scientists know how to manipulate genes sufficiently, there is danger that they will start engineering humans. Parents will want not only a healthy baby, but they will want to choose hair and eye color, height, personality, and other qualities affected by genes. Adults will want the baldness gene, the weak muscle gene, and the fat gene fixed. And this simply isn't right.

It isn't right morally, and it isn't right scientifically. Journalist Patricia J. Williams writes that artificial perfection is unhealthy: "I can't help entertaining the possibility that building Barbie and/or her dream life over and over again . . . is a way of going against a basic life force."[7] From the study of plants and animals, scientists know that species with diversity thrive. Dr. Kim Hooper, from California's Environmental Protection Agency, says, "It's like investing all your money in one stock. The benefit may be a higher yield for a time, but all it takes is one pesticide-resistant insect to wipe you out. Diverse populations survive better."[8]

Cautions

Dr. W. French Anderson, one of the first and best-known gene therapists, sums up the case for caution in gene therapy:

Medicine is a very inexact science. We understand roughly how a simple gene works. . . . Yet we have only limited understanding of how a body organ develops into the size and shape it does. . . . Even though we do not understand how a thinking, loving, interacting organism can be derived from its molecules, we are approaching the time when we can change some of those molecules. . . . What if in our innocent attempts to improve our genetic make-up, we alter [another important gene]? Could we test for the alteration? Certainly not at present. If we caused a problem that would affect the individual or his or her offspring, could we repair the damage? Certainly not at present.[9]

Until problems like these can be reliably solved, we should not count on gene therapy to give us perfect health.

1. Gina Maranto, *Quest for Perfection: The Drive to Breed Better Human Beings.* New York: Scribner, 1996, p. 272.

2. Gretchen Vogel, "From Science Fiction to Ethics Quandary," *Science,* September 19, 1997, p. 1753.

3. Quoted in Helen Thorpe, "Cancer Patience," *Texas Monthly,* January 1997, p. 86.

4. Thorpe, "Cancer Patience," p. 84.

5. Quoted in Maranto, *Quest for Perfection,* p. 272.

6. Quoted in Diane M. Gianelli, "'Enhancement' Gene Therapy Raises a New Ethical Dilemma," *American Medical News,* October 6, 1997, p. 4.

7. Patricia J. Williams, "I a Child and Thou a Lamb," *Nation,* February 2, 1998, p. 8.

8. Quoted in Williams, "I a Child and Thou a Lamb," p. 8.

9. Quoted in Maranto, *Quest for Perfection,* pp. 273–74.

CHAPTER 4

Cloning

"Allowing scientists to continue to experiment with human cloning can only lead to a . . . dangerous society in which people are no longer valued for themselves." ⁻

Human Cloning Should Be Banned

On March 4, 1997, President Bill Clinton issued an executive order. The president's command related to an issue few people thought would need to be addressed in our lifetimes. Mr. Clinton ordered that no federal funds be used to pay for human cloning research. Because federal money is the main source of financing for much of the scientific research done in the United States, this was a very serious position for the president to take. What led him to this stance was an announcement a week earlier by a Scottish embryologist, Dr. Ian Wilmut. Wilmut's announcement turned the world of science fiction into a frightening world of science fact.

Wilmut and a small team of scientists at the Roslin Institute near Edinburgh, Scotland, told the world that they had produced the first successful cloned mammal. The result of their accomplishment was a six-month-old lamb named Dolly. They created Dolly from a single cell from her mother's udder. Dolly was the first mammal to be an exact copy of another.

Wilmut was not the first scientist to attempt cloning. In fact, cloning technology has been used for decades in agriculture. Many food plants that grow today are the result of successful cloning practices. Likewise, scientists had experimented with

Dolly was the first mammal ever to be cloned. Many people fear that the technique will be extended to humans.

cloning small creatures—rats and frogs, for example. But none of the products of these experiments lived for more than a few days. Now Wilmut had proved it was possible to clone large animals— much closer to humans than mice and frogs—and to produce a living, healthy animal.

President Clinton and many others correctly saw this news as a dangerous hint of things that could happen if this kind of experimentation was allowed to continue. If a scientist could clone a sheep, why not a person? Jean Bethke Elshtain, who often writes about ethical issues, stated that "the President acted decisively and boldly, and what's more, rightly, when he called for a moratorium on all cloning experiments involving humans. . . . We—we humans, that is—should be haunted, by Dolly and all the Dollies to come."[1]

Violating Human Uniqueness

Why is the thought of cloning a human being so frightening? For one thing, cloning violates the very idea of being human. As President Clinton stated in his executive order, "Each human life is unique, born of a miracle that reaches beyond laboratory science."[2] Clones are not unique; they are reproductions of an original. And reproductions simply aren't as valuable as the original.

Some people have pointed out that cloning technology would allow the creation of replicas of the most gifted people in society. A dozen Einsteins would advance science beyond its wildest dreams; a dozen Michael Jordans would make the most amazing basketball teams one could ever imagine. But as Elshtain points out,

If there were basketball teams fielding Jordans against Jordans, we wouldn't be able to recognize the one, the only, Michael Jordan. It's like suggesting that forty Mozarts are better than one. There would be no Mozart if there were forty Mozarts. We know the singularity of the one, the extraordinary genius—a Jordan, a Mozart—because they stand apart from and above the rest. Absent that irreducible singularity, their gifts and glorious accomplishments would mean nothing. They would be the norm, the commonplace.[3]

Altering Our View of Humanity

Secondly, cloning will change how human beings view themselves. Newspaper columnist Cecil Johnson writes, "It is not a hysterical reaction to suggest [that] unrestrained human cloning and the moral acceptance of the practice could lead to the utter devaluation of the individual human being."[4]

If human cloning is allowed, people will gradually lose the belief that each individual is a valuable member of society; instead, humans will see themselves as products or commodities. Changing the "style" of a human will be as commonplace as changing the style of the latest exercise shoe. As Johnson says, "The temptation to eliminate the randomness from human selection, to create physically perfect specimens, and to custom-design people to fit society's economic, social, and cultural roles, could become irresistible."[5]

A New Caste System

Third, this changing view of humanity will eventually lead to the creation of a new caste system. India has been struggling for many decades to rid itself of a social system in which every individual is assigned at birth to a certain caste, or class, because of where and to whom they are born. The lowest caste in India is known as the untouchables. Cloning will lead other societies to create their own system in which the more "perfect" humans, by the day's fashion, will have privileges and prestige, while those who are imperfect or less fashionable will become "untouchables."

President Clinton has said that "creating a child through this new method ι . . . could lead to misguided and malevolent attempts to select certain traits, even to create certain kinds of children—to make our children objects rather than cherished individuals."[6] An individual could choose to have a clone of himself or herself instead of developing a relationship with a partner, having children in a natural way, and raising them in a loving family.

Today, people can go to a sperm bank and choose to use the sperm of a certain type of man—tall and blonde, athletic or musical, brilliant or average. They can then use the man's sperm to combine with a woman's egg. They hope the child that results will have some or all of the traits of the anonymous man whose sperm they chose. Even so, because the sperm is mixed with the woman's egg, and because some traits are stronger than others, they will end up with a unique child who may be more like the sperm father or the mother—or neither.

Only a few people choose this method of having a baby. But what if people could go to a clone bank and use a cell from a popular movie star, a dazzling athlete, or a brilliant scientist to create a clone? There would be no mystery involved. The resulting baby would be an exact copy of the person whose cell they used. Instead of having a baby, this would be more like going shopping for a new car or a new pair of shoes. People would be looking for the best or highest status product, not for a child to love.

Author John Garvey quotes Richard McCormick of the University of Notre Dame: "To attempt to create people with specific characteristics is to make single or multiple aspects of being human more important than the 'beautiful whole that is the human person.'" Garvey continues: "The real danger is the way the process moves us ever closer to the idea of the human being as product or property."[7]

To those who think that could never happen, Dr. Gerald Klassen says, "It is frightening how easily people can be subverted to evil purposes."[8] Klassen, a bioethicist and professor of medicine at Dalhousie University in Halifax, Canada, points to the medical experiments in Nazi Germany as an example of how easily this could take place. And history shows that civilization after civilization has enslaved peoples they considered inferior. There is no guarantee that this cannot happen again.

Dehumanizing Society

Allowing scientists to continue to experiment with human cloning can only lead to a dark and dangerous society in which people are no longer valued for themselves, but only for how they fit the particular styles that society believes it needs. People would become dehumanized, less humane. They would no longer care so much when a loved one died, because they could just as easily love their clone. No good can come of continuing this sorry trend. Human cloning should be banned.

1. Jean Bethke Elshtain, "Ewegenics," *New Republic*, March 31, 1997, p. 25.

2. Quoted in "To Clone or Not to Clone?" *Christian Century*, March 19, 1997, p. 286.

3. Elshtain, "Ewegenics," p. 25.

4. Cecil Johnson, "Cloning: Killing the Mystery of Humanity," Knight-Ridder Tribune News Service, January 27, 1998.

5. Johnson, "Cloning: Killing the Mystery of Humanity."

6. Quoted in Diane M. Gianelli, "Cloning Ban May Hinder Research," *American Medical News*, October 20, 1997, p. 4.

7. John Garvey, "The Mystery Remains: What Cloning Can't Reproduce," *Commonweal*, March 28, 1997, p. 6.

8. Quoted in Barry Came, "The Prospect of Evil," *Maclean's*, March 10, 1997, p. 59.

"Scary science fiction scenarios [about human cloning] are just that—fiction."

Human Cloning Should Not Be Banned

When the world learned that a team of Scottish researchers had successfully cloned an adult sheep, experts of all kinds immediately started shouting about the dangers of this technology. Once a large animal had been cloned, people began to worry about the possibilities—and dangers—of cloning human beings. They worried that human individuals would lose their value to society and that ruthless dictators would take over the world with armies of clones. These worries are baseless. Scary science fiction scenarios are just that—fiction. Even if human cloning should become practical (it is not practical today), it is likely that the benefits will outweigh the drawbacks. Listen to Harold Shapiro, president of Princeton University and chairman of the Federal Bioethics Advisory Commission:

> I have to admit that it [Scottish embryologist Dr. Ian Wilmut's successful cloning of a sheep] is a startling event that poses a host of questions, but at the same time, I have every confidence that we'll be able to do something to keep it under control. . . . The chances are this entire affair is going to end up producing a lot more benefits than costs.[1]

Shapiro points out that we have learned to control much more dangerous technology, such as nuclear weapons and poison gas. He rightly believes that we have little to fear by continuing to explore this relatively new area of scientific research and experimentation.

No Threat to the Individual

Many people, like newspaper columnist Cecil Johnson, believe that if we were to allow human cloning, society would lose its "complexity and produce cookie-cutter humanity. . . . Human life will lose both its mystery and its meaning."[2] But is this really true?

People who fear that cloning will remove all human individuality are wrong. They assume that a clone will be an exact replica in every way of the being from which its original cell came. But there's more to human beings than cells, genes, and DNA. Robert Wright, a writer for *Time* magazine, points out two important facts: First, "the world is already chock-full of virtual clones. My next-door neighbor—or the average male anywhere on the globe—is a 99.9 percent accurate genetic

NO. YOU SEE HERE. YOUR RESEARCH GRANT CALLS FOR YOU TO PRODUCE THE FIRST HUMAN CLONE. C-L-O-N-E.

Thornhill © '97 North County Times

copy of me."[3] Even so, Wright's next-door neighbor is dissimilar from him in almost every respect except that of being male: If you take any two men, or women, one may like basketball; the other hates it. One is kind and generous; another is crabby and stingy. One is tall and heavy; another is short and slight. One has five children; another is unable to have any. Wright suggests that most, if not all, of these differences would remain even if the two neighbors were actually clones and not just 99.9 percent similar.

Second, Wright says, "Many of the genes we share empower the environment to shape behavior and thus make us different from one another. Nature has preserved these 'malleability genes' because they adroitly tailor character to circumstance."[4] In other words, a large part of who we are comes from our environment—how we are treated by our family and community; whether we're the first child, the third, or an only child; whether our family is rich or poor, well educated or illiterate; whether we contract a life-threatening illness when we are a child; and on and on. Despite the biological cells we have in common, our life experience will be made up of enough different factors that we will be an entirely different individual from anyone else. Thus, even if a family chooses a clone of Michael Jordan as their child, they won't get a Michael Jordan. They *will* get a very tall, athletic male, but he is unlikely to have many personality traits in common with Michael Jordan because his life environment will have been entirely different—he may not even like basketball!

Wright's argument can be born out by looking at identical twins. They are, in a very real sense, clones. Yet they are identical only in appearance—and many times their individual tastes cause them to do things so they won't even *look* alike.

Dictators by the Dozen

Another commonly expressed fear is that people who are wealthy and powerful will clone themselves, thus guaranteeing that their power will continue even after their deaths. Or the clones of cruel dictators will perpetuate brutal regimes. It's true that people like this might look to cloning as a way to preserve their power. Yet the likelihood of things turning out the way they wish is small. If we think again about all the factors that influence the way a person turns out, we can easily see that the dictator's clones may be nothing like him or her at all.

Rudy Baum, managing editor of *Chemical & Engineering News*, points out that humans have always challenged, played with, and warped the laws of nature. It is a natural part of being human to want to understand and control as much of the world around oneself as possible. Baum asks and answers, "Will humans use cloning wisely? Not always, but for the most part, I think they will. The vast majority of us don't want to create carbon copies of ourselves. That alone makes bans on human cloning research unnecessary and counterproductive."[5]

Likely Benefits

When we think about prohibiting work on human cloning technology, we should also be aware of the many benefits we will lose. An editorial in the *Economist*, a weekly British magazine, states: "Many technologies that seemed pointless or dangerous when first mooted ended up by adding to the sum of human happiness. The worst thing that could happen now would be for the world to catch such a fright at the prospect of human clones that much promising work . . . is robbed of funding or banned outright."[6]

Cloning will be most obviously beneficial in the medical field, enabling more reliable study of disease and treatments. It will give scientists a better understanding of the very process of life. It will be another, more efficient way to enable infertile couples to have biological children. But perhaps most important of all are the benefits we don't yet know about. Nicole Noyes, a writer for *Cosmopolitan*, asserts:

> [The] main point in scientific research [is that] one idea sparks another, and every time we set out to accomplish a new goal, it leads to countless other findings. . . .

Think about the first time we put a man on the moon. True, the actual event probably didn't benefit you directly. But you needn't look any farther than your own car to find extralight, extrasafe metals that are just one of the everyday benefits derived from NASA's research. Likewise, pursuing the study of human cloning may spin off . . . [breakthroughs] as yet undreamed of.[7]

1. Quoted in Barry Came, "The Prospect of Evil," *Maclean's*, March 10, 1997, p. 59.

2. Cecil Johnson, "Cloning: Killing the Mystery of Humanity," Knight-Ridder/Tribune News Service, January 27, 1998.

3. Robert Wright, "Can Souls Be Xeroxed?" *Time*, March 10, 1997, p. 73.

4. Wright, "Can Souls Be Xeroxed?" p. 73.

5. Rudy Baum, "Playing God," *Chemical & Engineering News*, March 24, 1997, p. 10.

6. "Fear of Cloning," *Economist*, January 17, 1998, p. 18.

7. Nicole Noyes, "Why Human Cloning Research Should Not Be Banned," *Cosmopolitan*, October 1997, p. 60.

APPENDIX

Excerpts from Original Documents Pertaining to Biomedical Technology

Document 1: Some Medical Advances Made Using Animals

Those who advocate the use of animals in research point to the many lifesaving medical advances that could not have been accomplished without the use of animal-based research. Here is a list of some of those advances up through the 1980s. Since that time, more breakthroughs have occurred as a result of animal-based research, including the cloning of disease-busting cells, organ transplantation, the development of drugs to combat cancer, AIDS, and other diseases.

Pre-1900	• Treatment of rabies, anthrax, beriberi (thiamine deficiency) and smallpox • Principles of infection control and pain relief • Management of heart failure
Early 1900s	• Treatment of histamine shock, pellagra (niacin deficiency) and rickets (Vitamin D deficiency) • Electrocardiography and cardiac catheterization
1920s	• Discovery of thyroxin • Intravenous feeding • Discovery of insulin—diabetes control
1930s	• Therapeutic use of sulfa drugs • Prevention of tetanus • Development of anticoagulants, modern anesthesia and neuromuscular blocking agents
1940s	• Treatment of rheumatoid arthritis and whooping cough • Therapeutic use of antibiotics, such as penicillin, aureomycin and streptomycin • Discovery of Rh factor • Treatment of leprosy • Prevention of diphtheria
1950s	• Prevention of poliomyelitis • Development of cancer chemotherapy • Open-heart surgery and cardiac pacemaker
1960s	• Prevention of rubella • Corneal transplant and coronary bypass surgery • Therapeutic use of cortisone

- Development of radioimmunoassay for the measurement of minute quantities of antibodies, hormones and other substances in the body.

1970s
- Prevention of measles
- Modern treatment of coronary insufficiency
- Heart transplant
- Development of non-addictive painkillers

1980s
- Use of cyclosporin and other anti-rejection drugs
- Artificial heart transplantation
- Identification of psychophysiological factors in depression, anxiety and phobias
- Development of monoclonal antibodies for treating disease

American Medical Association, *Use Of Animals in Biomedical Research*, 1989.

Document 2: The Evolution of Animal Use in Research

At various times throughout medical research history, people have become alarmed at the ways animals have been used. The following is a brief history of the efforts to protect animals.

1822 British Anticruelty Act introduced by Richard Martin, who later founded the RSPCA (Royal Society for the Prevention of Cruelty to Animals)

1859 Charles Darwin publishes the theory of evolution

1866 Henry Bergh founds ASPCA (American Society for the Prevention of Cruelty to Animals)

1876 British Anticruelty to Animals Act regulates animal experimentation

1885 Louis Pasteur develops rabies vaccine

1891 Diptheria antitoxin produced from animal serum

1951 Christine Stevens founds Animal Welfare Institute in U.S.

1952 Jonas Salk develops killed-virus polio vaccine

1953 Albert Sabin develops live, attenuated polio vaccine

1954 Humane Society of the U.S. founded

1959 William M.S. Russell and Rex L. Burch state the "three R's" of animal experimentation (replace, reduce, refine)

1966 Animal Welfare Act (AWA) passed in the U.S.

1969 Dorothy Hegarty founds Fund for the Replacement of Animals in Medical Experiments in the U.K.

1970 Amendments to AWA cover warm-blooded animals and require pain relief

1975 Peter Singer publishes animal-liberation policy (*Animal Liberation:*

A New Ethics for Our Treatment of Animals)
1981   Center for Alternatives to Animal Testing founded in U.S.
1985   Amendments to AWA result from exposé of shocking conditions and animal abuse in Silver Spring, Maryland, and University of Pennsylvania laboratories
1992   European Center for the Validation of Alternative Methods founded
1993   First World Congress on Alternatives held in the U.S.
1996   Second World Congress on Alternatives held in Maryland

"The Evolution of Animal Use in Research," adapted from *Scientific American*, February 1997.

Document 3: Animal Tests Saved My Life

The author of the following article provides a dramatic example of how animal-based research saved his life.

Right now there are about 30,000 Americans waiting for a lifesaving organ transplant. Every day more names are added to this list of desperate people. Among the newcomers are bound to be some of those who carry the protest signs or write the letters. It is one thing to come up with catchy phrases charging animal abuse; it may be quite another to die because your efforts at propaganda have been successful.

Animal organs can help fill the need. True, the medical problems of animal-to-human transplants have not yet been solved. But for at least 10 years, the problems of human-to-human transplants were not solved, either.

It may be tough for these well-meaning people to reverse themselves. But it will be tougher for them to carry their signs outside a hospital where a friend, or the child of a friend, is dying.

Richard Pothier, "Animal Tests Saved My Life," *Newsweek*, February 1, 1993.

Document 4: Animal Welfare Act

PETA (People for the Ethical Treatment of Animals) wants to see animal-based research ended. Its leaders claim that the Animal Welfare Act of 1966 does not adequately protect animals.

The Animal Welfare Act is the meager federal law covering some areas of animal use. It was passed in 1966 and has been amended three times, most recently in December 1985. The U.S. Department of Agriculture (USDA) is responsible for its enforcement.

What places or businesses does the Animal Welfare Act cover?

The Act covers research facilities; dog and cat breeders and dealers; zoos, circuses and roadside menageries; and transporters of animals. The Act does not cover pet stores, state and county fairs, livestock shows, rodeos, dog and cat shows or "exhibitions intended to advance agricultural arts and sciences."

Does the Act cover all animals?

No. Technically, the Act covers any warm-blooded animals used in experiments, exhibits or for companionship. However, the USDA excludes "birds, rats and mice, and horses and other farm animals used or intended for food or fiber." This means, for example, that horses used in experiments are covered by the Act but horses used at rodeos are not. It also means that although rats and mice suffer and die by the millions in often painful experiments, they receive no protection at all from the Animal Welfare Act!

Does the Animal Welfare Act protect animals from cruelty?

Not necessarily. Contrary to popular belief, the Animal Welfare Act mainly regulates housekeeping standards, not actual experiments, activities or procedures, no matter how cruel or exploitative. The Act sets minimum standards for cage sizes, feeding, watering, sanitation and basic care, but ironically does not define many of these requirements and leaves them open to interpretation, which leaves animals open to abuse. The Act allows experimenters to withhold anesthetics at their discretion, denying some animals even basic pain relief.

Is the Act effectively enforced?

No. The Act's enforcement takes low priority at the USDA, and its budget and number of inspectors are woefully inadequate. A 1985 U.S. General Accounting Office study showed that most animal research facilities are inspected only once a year, and some are not inspected at all. The USDA also has trouble inspecting circuses and other operations that stay on the move. Some of the Act's 1985 amendment provisions, including improved conditions for primates, still have not been enacted.

Adapted from the People for the Ethical Treatment of Animals (PETA) brochure *Animal Welfare Act* (no date) by permission of PETA.

Document 5: Experimentation Facts

PETA has fought long and hard to eliminate the use of animals in medical and other research. Here are five facts PETA thinks people should know about animal experimentation.

- 60 to 100 million animals are killed annually in U.S. laboratories, in everything from burn and starvation experiments to weaponry testing and space research. Another 14 million plus are killed in product tests.
- In some states, pounds surrender dogs and cats to laboratories. "Bunchers" pick up strays, purchase litters, and/or trap and steal animals to sell for experiments.
- Outdated laws require that all drugs be tested on animals. Even so, more than half the prescription drugs approved by the FDA between 1976 and 1985 had to be relabeled or withdrawn from the market because of serious side effects. Cosmetics and household products are

not required to be tested on animals.

- Sophisticated research methods, such as computer models, cell cultures, and human clinical and epidemiological studies are more accurate, less expensive, and less time-consuming than animal experiments.
- More than 400 cosmetics and household product companies have announced permanent bans on animal testing. Many companies have *never* performed tests on animals.

"Animal Liberation," PETA, 1995.

Document 6: Animal Experiments Reach New Heights

As space programs have developed, so has the use of animals to study the effects of space travel on living organisms. The following article describes research done on the 1998 space shuttle Columbia.

Columbia's astronauts conducted the most complex animal dissections ever done in orbit Saturday, removing the brains of four rats so scientists can see how the nervous system changes in weightlessness.

Scientists say the only way to know precisely how the nervous system adapts and develops without gravity is to remove and preserve body parts in orbit. The only other time animals were dissected on a space shuttle was in 1993.

By the end of the Columbia's two-week Neurolab mission, 47 rodents are to be dissected, out of the total of 170 mice and rats carried into orbit Friday.

The job isn't nearly as messy in weightlessness as one might suspect. The animals are beheaded one at a time with a tiny guillotine or given an anesthetic overdose in a sealed laboratory chamber that has glovelike openings for astronauts' hands. Pads are folded over each animal to prevent body parts from floating away in the chamber. If something does float away, an astronaut can simply reach up with gauze and grab it.

It's a two-person job, which went to the Columbia's two doctors, Dave Williams and Jay Buckey Jr. Not only did they have to remove the rats' brains, they had to separate various sections of the brains and preserve them for post-flight study. The crew said everything went well.

Nine of the 18 pregnant mice will be dissected by the astronauts today, a much simpler procedure since the fetuses will be preserved whole. The remaining mice will be killed and dissected later in the flight, along with 25 other rats, most of them babies.

Most of the 152 rats launched on the Columbia will be killed and dissected once they're back on Earth, as will all of the 135 snails and 229 swordtail fish. Also flying on Neurolab, the most in-depth neurological research mission to date: four oyster toadfish and 1,514 crickets, some of them also destined for post-landing dissection.

The animals aren't the only ones being poked and prodded. Eleven of the 26 neurological experiments involve the shuttle's crew.

Marcia Dunn, "Animal Experiments Reach New Heights as Astronauts Dissect Rodents Aboard Shuttle," *St. Paul Pioneer Press*, April 19, 1998. Reprinted by permission of the Associated Press.

Document 7: The Nuremberg Code

The Nuremberg Code evolved from the shocking revelations of cruel medical experiments conducted on human beings by Nazi doctors during World War II.

1. The voluntary consent of the human subject is absolutely essential.

   This means that the person involved should have legal capacity to give consent; should be so situated as to be able to exercise free power of choice, without the intervention of any element of force, fraud, deceit, duress, overreaching, or other ulterior form of constraint or coercion; and should have sufficient knowledge and comprehension of the elements of the subject matter involved as to enable him to make an understanding and enlightened decision. This latter element requires that before the acceptance of an affirmative decision by the experimental subject there should be made known to him the nature, duration, and purpose of the experiment; the method and means by which it is to be conducted; all inconveniences and hazards reasonably to be expected; and the effects upon his health or person which may possibly come from his participation in the experiment.

   The duty and responsibility for ascertaining the quality of the consent rests upon each individual who initiates, directs, or engages in the experiment. It is a personal duty and responsibility which may not be delegated to another with impunity.

2. The experiment should be such as to yield fruitful results for the good of society, unprocurable by other methods or means of study, and not random and unnecessary in nature.

3. The experiment should be so designed and based on the results of animal experimentation and a knowledge of the natural history of the disease or other problem under study that the anticipated results will justify the performance of the experiment.

4. The experiment should be so conducted as to avoid all unnecessary physical and mental suffering and injury.

5. No experiment should be conducted where there is an a priori reason to believe that death or disabling injury will occur; except, perhaps, in those experiments where the experimental physicians also serve as subjects.

6. The degree of risk to be taken should never exceed that determined by the

humanitarian importance of the problem to be solved by the experiment.

7. Proper preparations should be made and adequate facilities provided to protect the experimental subject against even remote possibilities of injury, disability, or death.

8. The experiment should be conducted only by scientifically qualified persons. The highest degree of skill and care should be required through all stages of the experiment of those who conduct or engage in the experiment.

9. During the course of the experiment the human subject should be at liberty to bring the experiment to an end if he has reached the physical or mental state where continuation of the experiment seems to him to be impossible.

10. During the course of the experiment the scientist in charge must be prepared to terminate the experiment at any stage, if he has probable cause to believe, in the exercise of the good faith, superior skill, and careful judgment required of him, that a continuation of the experiment is likely to result in injury, disability, or death to the experimental subject.

Document 8: What Are Clinical Trials About?

Researchers are often looking for volunteers to participate in clinical trials of new drugs and therapies. The following is an excerpt from a government pamphlet that discusses what clinical trials are.

What Is a Clinical Trial?

In cancer research, a clinical trial is a study conducted with cancer patients, usually to evaluate a new treatment. Each study is designed to answer scientific questions and to find new and better ways to help cancer patients.

The search for good cancer treatments begins with basic research in laboratory and animal studies. The best results of that research are tried in patient studies, hopefully leading to findings that may help many people.

Before a new treatment is tried with patients, it is carefully studied in the laboratory. This research points out the new methods most likely to succeed, and, as much as possible, shows how to use them safely and effectively. But this early research cannot predict exactly how a new treatment will work with patients.

With any new treatment there may be risks as well as possible benefits. There may also be some risks that are not yet known. Clinical trials help us find out if a promising new treatment is safe and effective for patients. During a trial, more and more information is gained about a new treatment, its risks, and how well it may or may not work.

Standard treatments, the ones now being used, are often the base for building new, hopefully better treatments. Many new treatments are designed on the basis of what has worked in the past, in efforts to improve on this.

Only patients who wish to, take part in a clinical trial. You may be interested in or asked to enter a trial. Learn as much as you can about the trial, before you make up your mind.

Why Are Clinical Trials Important?

Advances in medicine and science are the results of new ideas and approaches developed through research. New cancer treatments must prove to be safe and effective in scientific studies with a certain number of patients before they can be made widely available.

Through clinical trials, researchers learn which approaches are more effective than others. This is the best way to test a new treatment. A number of standard treatments were first shown to be effective in clinical trials. These trials helped to find new and better treatments. . . .

What Are Important Questions To Ask About a Clinical Trial?

If you are thinking about taking part in a clinical trial, here are some important questions to ask:

- What is the purpose of the study?
- What does the study involve? What kinds of tests and treatments? (Find out what is done and how it is done.)
- What is likely to happen in my case with, or without, this new research treatment? (What may the cancer do and what may this treatment do?)
- What are other choices and their advantages and disadvantages? (Are there standard treatments for my case and how does the study compare with them?)
- How could the study affect my daily life?
- What side effects could I expect from the study? (There can also be side effects from standard treatments and from the disease itself.)
- How long will the study last? (Will it require an extra time commitment on my part?)
- Will I have to be hospitalized? If so, how often and for how long?
- Will I have any costs? Will any of the treatment be free?
- If I am harmed as a result of the research, what treatment would I be entitled to?
- What type of long-term followup care is part of the study? . . .

What Kinds of Clinical Trials Are There?

There are many kinds of clinical trials. They range from studies of ways to prevent, detect and diagnose, control and treat cancer, to studies of the psychological impact of the disease and ways to improve the patient's comfort and quality of life (including pain control).

Most cancer clinical trials deal with new treatments. These treatments often involve surgery, radiation therapy (the use of X-rays, neutrons or other types of cell-destroying radiation), and chemotherapy (the use of anticancer drugs). Alone, or in combination, these types of treatments can cure many cancer patients and prolong the lives of many others. A fairly new area of cancer treatment is biological therapy—the use of biologicals (substances produced by the body's own cells) and biological response modifiers (substances that affect the body's natural defense systems against disease).

How Are Trials Divided Into Phases?

Clinical trials are carried out in phases, each designed to find out certain information. Patients may be eligible for studies in different phases depending on their general condition and the type and stage of their cancer. More patients take part in the later phases of studies than in the earlier ones.

In a Phase I study, a new research treatment is given to a small number of patients. The researchers must find the best way to give a new treatment and how much of it can be given safely. They watch carefully for any harmful side effects. The research treatment has been well tested in laboratory and animal studies but no one knows how patients will react. Phase I studies may involve significant risks for this reason. They are offered only to patients whose cancer has spread and who would not be helped by other known treatments. Phase I treatments may produce anticancer effects, and some patients have been helped by these treatments.

Phase II studies determine the effect of a research treatment on various types of cancer. Each new phase of a clinical trial depends on and builds on information from an earlier phase. If a treatment has shown activity against cancer in Phase II, it moves to Phase III. Here it is compared with standard treatment to see which is more effective. Often researchers use standard therapy as the base to design new, hopefully better treatments. Then in Phase III, the new treatment is directly compared to the old one. In Phase IV studies, the new research treatment becomes part of standard treatment in patient care. For example, a new drug that has been found effective in a clinical trial may then be used together with other effective drugs, or with surgery and/or radiation therapy.

How Are Clinical Trials Conducted?

The doctors who conduct a clinical trial follow a carefully designed treatment plan called a "protocol." This spells out what will be done and why. Studies are planned to safeguard the medical and psychological health of patients as well as to answer research questions.

Some clinical trials test one research treatment in one group of patients. Other trials compare two or more treatments in separate groups of patients who are similar in certain ways, such as the extent of their disease. This way, the treatment groups are alike and the results from each can validly be compared.

One of the groups may receive standard (the most accepted) treatment so the new treatments can be directly compared to it. The group receiving the standard treatment is called the "control" group. For example, one group of patients (the control group) may receive the usual surgical treatment for a certain cancer, while another patient group with the same type of cancer may receive surgery plus radiation therapy to see if this improves disease control.

Sometimes, no standard treatment yet exists for certain cancer patients. In drug studies for such cases, one group of patients might receive a new drug and the control group, none. But no patient is placed in a control group without treatment if there is any known treatment that would benefit that patient. The control group is followed as often and carefully as the "treatment" group.

One of the ways to prevent the bias of a patient or doctor from influencing study results is "randomization." If a patient agrees to be randomized, this means he or she is selected by chance to be in one group or another. The researchers do not know which treatment is best. From what is known at the time, any one of the treatments chosen could be of equal benefit to the patient.

If the treatment in a trial is not helping the patient, the patient's doctor can decide to take him or her out of the study. Of course, the patient can decide to leave, as well, and still receive other available care. There are regular reviews of the results of a trial and the information is shared. This is important, because if a treatment is found to be too harmful or not effective, it is stopped. Also, when there is firm evidence that one method is better than the others in a study, the trial is stopped and all patients in the trial are given the benefit of the new information. Such information may help present and future patients.

Throughout a clinical study, a patient's personal doctor will be kept informed of the patient's progress. Patients are encouraged to maintain contact with their referring doctors.

"What Are Clinical Trials About? A Booklet for Patients with Cancer," National Institutes of Health, 1996.

Document 9: Prisoners of Research

History is replete with examples of unethical use of human beings in medical research. The following article is the account of one such incident.

It was 1951 when the father of Retin-A first came to Holmesburg Prison.

The 1,200 inmates of Philadelphia's gloomiest jail were plagued by an outbreak of athlete's foot, and the prison pharmacist had asked Dr. Albert Kligman, a University of Pennsylvania dermatologist, to take a look.

Imagine the researcher's thrill as he stepped into the aging prison, hundreds of men milling around.

"All I saw before me were acres of skin," Kligman told a newspaper reporter in 1966. "It was like a farmer seeing a field for the first time."

He had stumbled on a bonanza.

Twenty years later, Allen Hornblum entered the Philadelphia Detention Center to teach an adult literacy course.

Fresh out of a master's program at Villanova University, Hornblum, then 23, was getting his first view of a tough and alien society in a noisy, claustrophobic, foul-smelling city jail.

One sight struck him as particularly strange: Scores of men, bare-chested in the heat, their backs, shoulders and arms striped with gauze pads and adhesive tape.

"The sight of that, quite frankly, never left my mind," said Hornblum, now 50 and at the end of a long "crusade"—his word—to piece together the full story of what those bandages implied. The result is his first book, "Acres of Skin: Human Experiments at Holmesburg Prison; A True Story of Abuse and Exploitation in the Name of Medical Science" (Routledge) .

The bandaged inmates were not, as Hornblum first thought, victims of some awful riot.

As guards and inmates told him, the prisoners were taking part in "per-fume experiments" conducted by doctors from the University of Penn-sylvania. They were renting their bodies for cash. And nobody seemed to think it unusual.

The experiments in Philadelphia's prisons had been going on for 20 years, under Kligman's tutelage: tests involving toothpaste, deodorant, shampoo, skin creams, detergents, liquid diets, eye drops, foot powders and hair dye, "seemingly benign," Hornblum writes, "but accompanied by constant biopsies and frequently painful procedures."

And there were other tests, Hornblum would later learn, involving mind-altering drugs, radioactive isotopes and dioxin.

Kligman, who is 82 and living in Philadelphia, became a wealthy man and a famous name in dermatology, the inventor of Retin-A, the acne cream and wrinkle-remover widely hailed as youth in a tube.

"The early human trials," Hornblum writes of Retin-A, were per-formed on the backs and faces of the Holmesburg inmates."

Kligman has denied doing anything wrong. "My use of paid prisoners as research subjects in the 1950s and 1960s was in keeping with this nation's standard protocol for conducting scientific investigations at that time," he said . . . in a two-sentence statement, one of the few he has made on the subject.

"To the best of my knowledge," Kligman added, "the result of those experiments advanced our knowledge of the pathogenesis of skin disease, and no long-term harm was done to any person who voluntarily partici-pated in the research program."

The experiments ended in 1974 as a wave of national publicity and con-gressional hearings put an end to most human experimentation involving populations such as prisoners and mental patients.

"It was chilling," Hornblum said in a recent interview, "to be in a totalitarian atmosphere, which a prison is, and to see minorities—the prison was about 85 percent black and there were very few high school graduates—to see all these people involved in some medical experiment about which they had a minimal amount of information.

"It just rubbed me raw."

The idea that an injustice had gone unaddressed nagged at Hornblum. Four years ago, the sometime college teacher and political adviser quit his job as chief of staff to Philadelphia Sheriff John Green. Without a book contract or a salary to fall back on, he plunged headlong into a welter of interviews, libraries and obscure documents, hoping to illuminate an era that had received very little light.

Hornblum is not the first critic to raise questions about the prison experiments. In 1979 the *Philadelphia Inquirer* disclosed that inmates had been used as guinea pigs to test whether mind-altering drugs were useful as Army weapons. In 1981 the paper reported that inmates had been dosed with dioxin to test the herbicide's effects on human health.

But Hornblum's account is the most extensive and detailed to date. He writes that inmates were told very little about the tests performed on them—in violation, Hornblum argues, of the Nuremberg Code adopted after World War II in reaction to Nazi medical atrocities. The code's first statement: "The voluntary consent of the human subject is absolutely essential."

Prisoners, Hornblum writes, were more than eager to gamble their health for pay. At Holmesburg, the going rate was $10 to $300, depending on the experiment—a fortune compared to the jail's wages of 15 cents or 25 cents a day.

Enter Kligman. Hornblum describes him as a brilliant and entrepreneurial scientist, a pioneer in his field, a man of brimming self-confidence who told students that rules don't apply to genius.

A common test was what inmates called a "patch test." Strips of hospital tape were stuck to an inmate's upper back, forming a grid with about 20 squares. On each square went a dab of lotion (skin cream, moisturizer, suntan lotion—a variety of products). Then came heat from a sunlamp. Doctors checked the skin for peeling, burning and blistering at different temperatures.

Withers Pond, a 79-year-old lifer, told Hornblum he once volunteered for a "gauze test." Without anesthetic, he lay on a table while two doctors cut two 1-inch incisions on each side of his lower back, inserted gauze pads into the wounds and then stitched him up, he said. Ten days later, doctors reopened one wound, removed the gauze pad and restitched him. They removed the other gauze pad 10 days later.

Pond never learned the purpose of the exercise, but he got $20. "Now I got these scars all over my back," he said.

A former inmate named Johnnie Williams told Hornblum that the mind-altering drugs he took as a Holmesburg research subject changed his personality; he went from small-time hood to violent criminal.

Hit by a car recently, Williams refused to go to a hospital.

"I'm paranoid about doctors," he told Hornblum. "I'm scared of 'em."

For all that, there are few documented cases of long-term injury to the estimated thousands of inmates who took part in the experiments. The main reason, according to Hornblum: Kligman destroyed the records when the program was killed in 1974.

Howard Goodman, "Prisoners of Research," *St. Paul Pioneer Press*, June 3, 1998. Reprinted with permission of Knight-Ridder/Tribune Information Services.

Document 10: A Brief History of Transplants

Only in the last forty-five years have doctors been able to successfully transplant organs from one person to another. Here are brief highlights of transplant surgery.

1933   First human-to-human kidney transplant (kidney never functioned).

1954   First successful kidney transplant from one twin to another with no anti-rejection drugs necessary. Dr. Joseph Murray, Brigham & Women's Hospital, Boston. (More kidney transplants between identical twins were performed immediately afterward, and some of those kidney recipients are still alive.)

1967   First successful liver transplant, Dr. Thomas Starzl, University of Colorado Health Sciences Center, Denver.

1967   World's first heart transplant, Dr. Christiaan Barnard, South Africa.

1968   First successful heart transplant in United States, Dr. Denton Cooley at Houston's St. Luke's Episcopal Hospital.

1968   Uniform Anatomical Gift Act passed, creating the "Donor Card" and allowing families to consent to or refuse donation. It also prohibited doctors attending the donor from participating in organ removal or transplantation.

1978   Uniform Brain Death Act passed, expanding for the first time the traditional definition of death. "Brain death" IS death.

1983   Cyclosporine, a revolutionary anti-rejection drug, approved for commercial use, sparking a huge increase in transplants.

1984   National Organ Transplant Act passed, prohibiting the sale of human organs and setting up a national transplant network to procure and distribute organs. The United Network for Organ Sharing received the federal contract to oversee the network starting in 1986.

1986   "Routine request" law passed, requiring hospitals to give families the opportunity to donate organs by asking them in appropriate cases.

Patty Reinert, "Final Decisions," *Houston Chronicle*, November 27, 1997.

Document 11: Need and Availability of Organs

Ever since organ transplantation has been possible, the need has far outstripped the availability of viable organs.

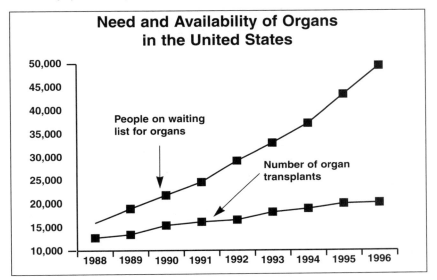

United Network for Organ Sharing.

Document 12: Uniform Donor Card

People who wish to donate their organs when they die fill out a Uniform Donor Card and keep it in their wallet. In some states, their driver's license may also indicate that they wish to be a donor. Additionally, donors should let their family and their physician know that this is their wish.

UNIFORM DONOR CARD

OF_____
(Print or type name of donor)

In the hope that I may help others, I hereby make this anatomical gift, if medically acceptable, to take effect upon my death. The words and marks below indicate my desires:

I give (a) ____ any needed organs or tissues
      (b) ____ only the following organs or tissues

_____
Specify the organ(s) or tissue(s)

for the purposes of transplantation, therapy, medical research or education;

      (c) ____ my body for anatomical study if needed.

Limitations or special wishes, if any:

_____

Signed by the donor and the following two witnesses in the presence of each other:

_____   _____
Signature of Donor   Date of Birth of Donor

_____   _____
Date Signed   City and State

_____   _____
Witness   Witness
    (Preferably next of kin)

This is a legal document under the Uniform Anatomical Gift Act or similar laws.

Document 13: Catch-22 for Patient

The impact of organ transplantation is not only medical. It also has a strong psychological impact on both donor and recipient. The following is the statement of a grateful recipient.

Given the gift of life, how can I repay my donor family, my surgeons and society?

I was just a kid, 12 years old. I wanted to be some kind of hero when I grew up. Most kids do. It was Mt. Horeb, Wis. German. English. Work hard. Stiff upper lip. Be a man. Even now those ethics scream out against this essay. It's hard for me to tell you about myself. Actually, it's also hard for me to be me. At 6 feet 2 inches and 220 pounds, I'm what they call a "strapping fellow." Maybe that's how I caught the eye of a Secret Service recruiter one day in college.

I had just voted for Ronald Reagan (my very first election) because of my anger for those trapped in the American Embassy in Iran. I wanted to do something. And now here was a guy telling me I could. I dropped my English major, substituted criminal justice and threw all my energy into applying for the Secret Service. It was a cold slap when the rejection letter came. If I hadn't been so naive I would have known my ambition was doomed from the start.

The recruiter hadn't noticed a certain something about me. That certain something has cost you, the taxpayer, hundreds of thousands of dollars. I would like to pay you back. There's a catch, though. Death is a risk I take if I get a job. Not from hazards in the workplace, but from hazards in the bureaucracy. What happened when I was just a kid of 12 was the diagnosis of juvenile diabetes. It didn't stop me from triple-lettering in sports as a teenager, but by my early 30s I needed new kidneys.

I got them, thanks to the kindness of a wonderful donor family and the skill of dedicated physicians. I also got a new pancreas. My diabetes was cured.

But transplants aren't covered by many private insurance carriers, and I didn't have several hundred thousand dollars of my own to pay for the ongoing procedures. So I, like thousands of other patients, was advised to deliberately impoverish myself in order to qualify for government medical benefits. When you've already flat-lined, gone blind in one eye and had three heart attacks, well, whatever they tell you makes sense. At that point your only career goal is to stay alive.

And alive I am. After dropping out of college for several years, I've finished my bachelor's degree, graduating two years to the day after receiving my new organs. My professors at Ottawa University in Arizona tell me they were shocked. I'm such a big, burly guy they had no idea I was a transplant patient.

But they learned the truth about me from my research paper. They also learned that any transplant's new life—not just mine—is frequently dominated by welfare.

There are now more than 20,000 whole-organ transplant recipients every year. This number doesn't include bone-marrow patients. As the technology improves there will be even more. The drugs I take daily to prevent organ rejection and other complications cost about $1,500 per month. Most of us, in what should be the most productive years of your lives, would like to trot these fabulous new organs to a work site. We'd be glad to pay taxes. It would be a privilege and a joy.

Instead, I know transplants (that's what we call ourselves) who work furtively at small projects payable in cash. Earnings of $260, if reported, would disrupt medical benefits. I know transplants who, on paper, are married. Each spouse has moved on to other relationships, but the insurance plan—now irreplaceable—is still intact.

How else do we cope? We hoard our drugs. We call R inventory. We keep any excess cataloged, stored and ready. This is our "cache of life" to guard against the day red tape chokes off those precious pills. "You need some cyclosporine? I've got extra," I've heard. Don't judge harshly, please. Until you have a foreign heart beating in your chest or someone else's liver washing your blood, you won't know how we feel.

So here's the question: now that we're alive, how do we get back into the swing of things? How do I get off welfare? Most mornings I go to a coffee shop nearby. I toy with my mug of joe and watch other men—construction guys—heading off to work. I look like I should be one of them. They probably think I am. The diabetes that began ravaging my body as a child makes that unrealistic, though. Sometimes I wonder just what I'm fit for. When my mind starts playing tricks like that, I remember my bachelor's thesis: "Some Psychological Consequences of Transplant Surgery." I wanted to know what happens to the mind while the kidneys, heart, liver and lungs are being replaced.

While I can't work construction, I am fit for quite a few things. With my background—I've worked as a patrolman, enforcing state-park laws while pursuing my original major, law enforcement—I would make a good investigator. I'm great with kids, having lettered in football, basketball and track in high school and coached several sports in public schools. I was a relief counselor in a boys' home. Now that I have a degree in psychology, I am qualified for any of those types of jobs, and my health wouldn't be a drawback. There are plenty of men who wouldn't be "fit" for construction. Why should my heart squeeze with envy as those fellows shuffle out of the coffee shop in the mornings? It does because they are leaving me behind. They are contributing.

You've probably heard this before, but people who have had a near-

death experience, as I have had, feel a need to help others. I didn't see
Elvis; I just slumped over. But those amazing doctors wouldn't give up.
And when I came back I felt that time was no longer my own. I had survived so much, surely this life of mine was a borrowed thing. I felt I should
make a difference.

My professors think I can accomplish that by telling my story. By call-
ing attention to the plight of the transplant. How odd it feels to use that
word, plight. We transplants are blessed. We were all—every single one—
supposed to be dead. But we really didn't mean to borrow so much. We're
ready to give back. We want to repay all our surgeons and donor families
and the miraculous society that made it all possible. We want to work!

Document 14: The Right Thing to Do

*Bone marrow is needed as much as organs such as kidneys, livers, and hearts. Just
as with donors of those other vital organs, the bone marrow donor undergoes physical and psychological trauma to give the gift of life. In the following article, the
author tells why she is glad she donated marrow, even though the recipient died
after only a year.*

I lost a friend recently. Her name was Mary. I never met her. I spoke to her
once, and we corresponded about a half dozen times over the past year.
That's it. On many levels, I did not know Mary at all, and yet we were con-
nected in a way that few people are. She was my recipient. I was her donor.
Our connection was bone marrow.

When I donated a blood sample and officially joined the National Bone
Marrow Registry, it just seemed like the thing to do. I saw a flier on a
streetside fruit stand. I did not know the person for whom the drive was
sponsored. I just went to a church hall where a temporary blood center had
been set up and gave a little blood. Painless. The nurse assistants told me
the chances were very slim that I would ever get called. But I did. I went
to give more blood for further antigen matching, and they told me again
it was unlikely that I would get called back. It took longer this time, but I
did. More tests, more matching. And then nothing for a while. Until the
call that told me that the "miracle match" had happened. Was I still willing to donate?

All this time I'd never really thought it would happen. Truthfully I did-
n't give it much thought at all. Now I had a decision to make, though it
really wasn't much of a decision. I knew in my heart all along what I would
do. The main-blood-center people gave me lots of information and lots of
physical tests to make sure that I was healthy. My husband was worried
more than I (he is in the medical field and knew more about every little

thing that could go wrong, no matter how remote). When all was said and done, I got the papers, the Consent to Donate, and I signed. The bottom line was, how could I not?

Shortly afterward I spent a couple of days in the hospital to donate the marrow. It wasn't the easiest thing I have ever done. There were some unexpected complications caused by the anesthesia, but I got through them. I experienced some discomfort from the marrow-removal procedure. People had told me ahead of time that it would feel like I'd taken a hard fall on the ice, landing on my butt. That was pretty accurate. But I'd given birth to two children, and by comparison the bone-marrow retrieval was a breeze, complications and all. Within two weeks I felt 80 percent fine; within a month it was like nothing had happened.

Physically, that is really the end of my part of the story. But I knew that somewhere there was a woman who was just starting her battle. When you donate marrow to an unrelated recipient, the bone-marrow registry really stresses the confidentiality of both the donor and the recipient. I knew my recipient was a female; I knew her physical problem and her age. That was it. No name, no location, nothing else. I wrote a short, unaddressed note that accompanied my marrow. A few weeks later, I received a note back. Actually it was a copy. Letters between donors and recipients are screened, and my contact at the blood center would "white out" any personal references and then make a copy to pass on. But I tell you, it was one of the most wonderful things I had ever read. It made the connection between us seem more real, more personal.

In subsequent months we wrote to each other a number of times. We even came up with code names since we did not like the impersonal greeting of "Dear Donor" or "Dear Recipient." I was Cleopatra (Cleo for short), and she was Joan (for Joan of Arc). In each letter we learned more about one another. It is amazing how much you can tell about yourself without giving any specific locations or names. Toward the end of the year we were each trying to sneak in hints about where we lived. She mentioned something about apple picking and fresh maple sugar (I was sure she was in Vermont), and I wrote about going to see a well-known Broadway musical, hoping she would guess I was in the New York area. We finally got caught by our respective contacts and had to keep our last letters more straightforward. I happily anticipated each letter "Joan" sent. It was fun to hear from her, and her letters gave me some hope that the marrow transplant was working.

Exactly one year after the transplant I got a call from the contact at my blood center. She had "Joan's" real name and address. Her name was Mary, a simple, wonderful name. She lived in New York state. So much for my Vermont guess. I was told that Mary was not at home; she was at the hospital where the transplant had occurred for her one-year checkup. Later on in the evening my husband answered the phone. He turned to me with a smile and said, "It's Joan of Arc. For you." We were finally voice to voice. We spoke for 20 minutes. It was wonderful! We filled in a lot of names and places for each other. We joked about appearing on television together— she wanted to do "Geraldo," I said it was "Rosie" or nothing. We decided we would make plans to meet when she returned from the hospital. She had a slight lung infection but was hoping to leave soon. When I got off the phone I thought of a million other things to ask, but I knew we would meet each other shortly. I sent off a Valentine's card with a picture of my children. It was a pleasure to write "Dear Mary."

One week from the day we spoke. I got another phone call. This time it was my contact. I knew right away something was wrong. Mary had died. But how could this be? We had spoken; we were going to get together. I didn't think it was going to be a fairy-tale ending, but not this. Not so soon. I cried and cried. For Mary, for myself, for her family, whom I didn't even know but who had been through so much.

A few days later my contact called back to see how I was doing. She told me I had given Mary a year she would not have had. She told me that Mary's family at least had the comfort of knowing that everything had been done, no stone left unturned, no "what if we had found a marrow match." I know all this, and I have no regrets. I was blessed with the opportunity to try to make a saving difference in someone's life. Most people are not given that chance. I feel fortunate. I wish that Mary and I could have become old friends, celebrating life. Instead, I lost a new friend, one that I will never forget.

Document 15: Porky Procedure

Scientists are constantly looking for ways to meet the growing need for organ transplants. Many researchers believe one of the best sources might be animals. The author of the following excerpt provides some basic information about these xenotransplants.

"You'll need a liver transplant," Dr. Zeno says. She scribbles quickly on her prescription pad and dates it: April 17, 2025. "Take this to the hospital pharmacy and we'll schedule the surgery for Friday morning."

The patient sighs—he's visibly relieved that his body will be rid of hepatitis forever.

"What kind of liver will it be?" he asks.

"Well, it's from a pig," Zeno replies. "But it will be genetically altered with your DNA. Your body won't even know the difference."

Obviously, this is science fiction. But according to some scientists, it could be a reality someday. An animal organ, probably from a pig, could be genetically altered with human genes to trick a patient's immune system into accepting it as its own flesh and blood.

Called "xenotransplants," such animal-to-human procedures would be lifesaving for the thousands of people waiting for organ donations. There have been about 30 experimental xenotransplants since the turn of the century. . . .

Today, human organ transplants are commonplace. For example, more than 10,000 Americans received kidney transplants last year, with a three-year life expectancy of more than 85 percent, according to the United Network for Organ Sharing (UNOS), an organization of transplant programs and laboratories in the United States. Under contract to the U.S. Department of Health and Human Services, UNOS administers a national organ network, and its members set policies for equitable organ allocation.

Surgeons have made great strides in perfecting transplant techniques, but two problems endure. First, there are never enough organs to go around. Second, once patients receive organs, it is a constant battle to keep their immune systems from rejecting them. Both problems may be eventually solved by xenotransplants and the genetic engineering techniques developed from such experiments.

Of all animals, baboons and pigs are the favored xenotransplant donors. Baboons are genetically close to humans, so they're most often used for initial experiments. Six baboon kidneys were transplanted into humans in 1964, a baboon heart into a baby in 1984, and two baboon livers into patients in 1992.

Although all the patients died within weeks after their operations, they did not die of organ rejection. Rather, they died of infections common to patients on immunosuppressive drugs.

One drawback to using baboons is that they harbor many viruses. They also reproduce slowly, carrying only one offspring at a time. Some people have raised ethical objections, especially since baboons are so similar to humans. They have human-like faces and hands and a highly developed social structure. Although it's conceivable that baboons could donate bone marrow without being killed, recent experiments have required extensive tissue studies, and the animals have been sacrificed.

For long-term use, pigs may be a better choice. Pigs have anatomies strikingly similar to that of humans. Pigs are generally healthier than most primates and they're extremely easy to breed, producing a whole litter of piglets at a time. Moral objections to killing pigs are fewer since they're slaughtered for food.

Pig organs have been transplanted to humans several times in the last few years. In 1992, two women received pig liver transplants as "bridges" to hold them over until human transplants were found. In one patient, the liver was kept outside the body in a plastic bag and hooked up to her main liver arteries. She survived long enough to receive a human liver. In the other patient, the pig liver was implanted alongside the old diseased liver, to spare the patient the rigors of removing it. Although that patient died before a human transplant could be found, there was some evidence that the pig liver had functioned for her.

By genetically altering pig livers, some scientists believe they can make a pig liver bridge more successful. In July 1995, FDA permitted the Duke University Medical Center to test genetically altered pig livers in a small number of patients with end-stage liver disease. The pig livers contained three human genes that will produce human proteins to counter the rejection process.

Rebecca D. Williams, "Organ Transplants from Animals: Examining the Possibilities," *FDA Consumer*, June 1966.

Document 16: Genetic Testing Pushes Buttons

One of the most pressing concerns about genetic testing is discrimination in the workplace. Here is what 332 people had to say about the subject.

As more employers consider the use of genetic testing, HR [Human Resources, or personnel] professionals should expect a variety of reactions—from fear to distrust and anger. Below are some common perceptions and concerns about genetic testing that were revealed in a study of 332 members of genetic support groups (all of whom had one or more of 101 different genetic disorders).

- Individuals who say they were asked about genetic diseases or disabilities on an application for health insurance: 40%

- People who claim they or a family member were refused health insurance as a result of a genetic condition in their family: 22%

- People who say they wouldn't want their insurer to know if they were tested and found to be at high risk of a genetic disorder: 83%

- Adults with a life insurance policy in the United States: 70%

- Those paying higher-than-standard premiums on a life insurance policy: 5%

- Individuals who claim they or a family member were denied a job or "let go" because of a genetic condition in the family: 13%

- People who say they were asked about genetic diseases or disabilities on a job application: 7%

- Those claiming they were denied or "let go" from a job due to genetic information: 3%

- Those who say they haven't revealed genetic information to their employers for fear of losing their jobs or insurance coverage: 17%

- Those refusing a genetic test for fear of discrimination: 9%

- Respondents claiming they've been genetically discriminated against: 43%

- Individuals who were asked about genetic diseases or disabilities on an application and then refused health insurance: 47%

Workforce, July 1997. Source: Human Genome Educational Model Project of Georgetown University Child Development Center and the Alliance of Genetic Support Groups, 1996.

Document 17: ACLU Urges Senate Committee

The American Civil Liberties Union is a dogged guardian of human rights. Alarmed at the discrimination complaints they received about genetic testing, they called upon the federal government to pass legislation guarding the rights of those who undergo genetic testing.

Saying that hundreds of men and women have already suffered serious discrimination after genetic testing, the American Civil Liberties Union today urged a Senate committee to provide privacy safeguards and protections against discrimination based on genetic conditions.

In testimony submitted to the Senate Labor and Human Resources Committee, the ACLU said that as the cost of genetic testing declines—and the number of conditions that can be tested for increases—genetic testing may become as common as drug testing. The committee today held a hearing to examine the privacy of individual genetic information.

Even at current levels of testing, the ACLU said that many individuals and families are experiencing discrimination. A 1996 Georgetown University study, for example, found that of 332 families belonging to genetic disease support groups, 22 percent said they had been refused health insurance and 13 percent said they had been fired from their jobs because of the perceived risks attributed to their genetic status.

And the numbers are rising. A 1982 federal survey found that 1.6 percent of companies used genetic testing for employment purposes. Last year, according to a similar survey conducted by the American Management Association, the number had increased to approximately 10 percent of employers.

"Legislation is the only way to address the growing trend of genetic discrimination," said Jeremy Gruber, the Legal Director of the ACLU's National Taskforce on Civil Liberties in the Workplace, who prepared today's testimony. "We know that individuals are already avoiding necessary and important testing for fear that their genetic information will be shared with employers and insurance companies."

Although most experts believe that the Americans with Disabilities Act provides some defense against genetic discrimination, Gruber said that current law provides no protection for the privacy of employees and does not prevent employers from obtaining genetic information.

"It is crucial that Congress place restrictions on the ability of employers and insurers to collect genetic information," Gruber said. "Without meaning privacy safeguards and protections against discrimination, the potential medical benefits of genetic testing will be lost as Americans avoid tests in fear of possible adverse consequences."

ACLU press release, May 21, 1998.

Document 18: NCI Fact Sheet

The National Cancer Institute, part of the National Institutes of Health, released a fact sheet about gene therapy. Here is an excerpt.

What is gene therapy and what are its objectives?

Recent advances in understanding and manipulating genes—the biological units of heredity—have set the stage for scientists to alter patients' genetic material to fight or prevent disease. One major goal of gene therapy is to supply cells with healthy copies of missing or flawed genes. This approach is revolutionary: Instead of giving a patient a drug to treat or control the symptoms of a genetic disorder, physicians attempt to correct the basic problem by altering the genetic makeup of some of the patient's cells.

Hundreds of major health problems are influenced by gene functions. In the future, gene therapy could be used to treat many of these conditions. Theoretically, it could also be used to alter germ cells (egg or sperm) in order to prevent a genetic defect from being transmitted to future generations. However, the possibility of germ-line gene therapy is beset by difficult ethical and social questions as well as technical obstacles.

Gene therapy could also be used as a drug delivery system. To accomplish this, a gene that produces a useful product would be inserted into the DNA of the patient's cells. For example, during blood vessel surgery, a gene that makes an anticlotting factor could be inserted into the DNA of cells lining blood vessels to help prevent dangerous blood clots from forming. Many other conditions might also lend themselves to treatment using this general approach.

As medicine operates increasingly on the molecular level, using gene therapy for drug delivery could save much effort and expense. It could shortcut the lengthy and complicated process of collecting large amounts of a gene's protein product, purifying the product, formulating it as a drug, and administering it to the patient.

However, gene therapy is still extremely new and highly experimental. The number of approved trials is small, and relatively few patients have been treated to date.

What are the basic steps involved in current gene therapy experiments?
In some current experiments, cells from the blood or bone marrow are removed from the patient and grown in the laboratory under conditions that encourage them to multiply. Then the desired gene is inserted into the cells with the help of a disabled virus, and the successfully altered cells are selected out, encouraged to multiply, and returned to the patient's body. In other cases, liposomes (fatty particles) or disabled viruses may be used to deliver the gene directly to cells within the patient's body. . . .

What is the process by which gene therapy experiments receive approval?
A proposed experiment, or protocol, must pass through at least two review boards at the scientists' institution and must be approved by that institution. The protocol must then be approved by the Recombinant DNA Advisory Committee (RAC) of the National Institutes of Health (NIH) and be signed by the NIH director. All protocols must also receive the approval of the U.S. Food and Drug Administration.

Why are there so many steps in this process?
Any experimentation in humans must be approached with great care. Gene therapy in particular is a very powerful technique, and it is relatively new. These factors make it necessary for scientists to take special precautions with gene therapy until they have gained more experience with this new technology. . . .

What major problems must scientists overcome before gene therapy becomes a common technique for treating disease?
As mentioned earlier, scientists need to learn how to isolate and insert curative genes into stem, or progenitor, blood cells, so they can treat immunologic and blood disorders.

Scientists also need to find easier and better ways of delivering genes to the body. To treat cancer, AIDS, and other diseases effectively with gene therapy, they need to develop vectors that can be injected directly into the patient. These vectors must then home in on appropriate target cells (e.g., cancer cells) throughout the body and successfully integrate the desired gene into the DNA of these cells.

New vectors are currently being tested. These include adenoviruses, which, unlike retroviruses, can transfer genetic material to nondividing cells, such as those found in the lungs; and liposomes, or fat droplets, which can adhere to some cells, including tumor cells, and insert genes into these cells.

Two other advances are needed: one or more ways to deliver genes consistently to a precise location in the patient's genetic material (thus diminishing the risk of inducing cancer during gene transfer), and the ability to ensure that transplanted genes are precisely regulated by the body's normal physiologic signals. Insulin is just one example of a protein that must be produced in the right amounts at the right times if it is to help rather than harm the patient.

Although scientists are working hard on these problems, it is impossible to predict when the various obstacles will be overcome. . . .

What impact is gene therapy likely to have on medicine in the future?
Gene therapy could redefine the practice of medicine in the next century. It should be a powerful tool for treating many of the more than 4,000 known genetic disorders, as well as heart disease, cancer, arthritis, and other illnesses.

Originally, even the proponents of gene therapy expected it to be limited largely to the treatment of hereditary disorders, such as cystic fibrosis or hemophilia. But scientists at NIH and elsewhere are now exploring not only the possibility of permanent cures for some of these obviously genetic diseases but also the treatment of an ever-broadening range of other illnesses, including heart disease, AIDS, and cancer.

These new treatments could add to the costs of health care. On the other hand, it is possible that gene therapy will eventually be used to prevent or cure diseases that now kill or disable millions of Americans. If so, it has the potential to revolutionize health care by enabling more people to remain productive members of society and by eliminating or reducing the need for costly medications and other treatments that ameliorate symptoms but do not cure disease.

"NCI Fact Sheet," National Cancer Institute, May 1998.

Document 19: Summary and Conclusions

The National Institutes of Health and U.S. Department of Health and Human Services established a task force to study genetic research, how it is conducted, and its ramifications. An excerpt from the group's report is printed here.

The Task Force recommends that the Secretary of Health and Human Services appoint an advisory committee on genetic testing to be instrumental in implementing the recommendations of this Task Force. The advisory committee or its designate should establish a system for determining which genetic tests require stringent scrutiny. If a test is likely to be used to predict future disease in healthy people, it is a candidate for stringent scrutiny, but not all predictive tests will necessarily require such scrutiny and other criteria are needed as well.

The Task Force wishes to highlight the following recommendations and to indicate the organizations primarily responsible for facilitating them:

(1) Protocols for the development of genetic tests that can be used predictively must receive the approval of an institutional review board (IRB) when subject identifiers are retained and when the intention is to make the test readily available for clinical use. Office for Protection of Research Risks (OPRR) in cooperation with the proposed Secretary's Advisory Committee is primarily responsible.

(2) Test developers must submit their validation and clinical utility data to external review as well as to interested professional organizations in order to permit informed decisions about routine use. Independent review should take place at both the local level (e.g., academic center or company), and at the national level by professional societies, consensus panels, federal agencies and other organizations before new tests become available for noninvestigational clinical use. The proposed Secretary's Advisory Committee should coordinate national efforts.

(3) The Task Force urges the newly created genetics subcommittee of the Clinical Laboratory Improvement Advisory Committee to consider the creation of a specialty of genetics which would encompass all predictive tests that satisfy criteria for stringent scrutiny. If only a subspecialty for DNA/RNA-based tests is feasible, the subcommittee must then address how to assure the quality of laboratories performing non-DNA/RNA predictive genetic tests. The agencies primarily responsible for administering CLIAC, Health Care Financing Administration (HCFA), and Centers for Disease Control (CDC) should take the lead in implementing this recommendation.

(4) The Task Force encourages the development of genetics curricula in medical school and residency training. In addition to these basic curricula, each specialty involved with the care of patients with disorders with significant genetic components should design relevant curricula for continuing education in genetics. Schools of nursing, public health, and social work need to strengthen and expand their training programs in genetics. The newly created National Coalition for Health Professionals Education in Genetics should greatly facilitate improving professional education in genetics.

(5) Hospitals and managed care organizations should require evidence of competence before permitting providers to order predictive stringent scrutiny genetic tests or to counsel about them. Implementation is at the local level. If accrediting organizations include a review of the management of selected genetic tests as part of their accreditation, there will be greater stimulus for local organizations to assure quality.

(6) Physicians who encounter patients with symptoms and signs of rare genetic diseases should have access to accurate information that will enable them to include such diseases in their differential diagnosis, to know where to turn for assistance in clinical and laboratory diagnosis, and to locate laboratories that test for rare diseases. The quality of laboratories providing tests for rare diseases must be assured, and a comprehensive system to collect data on rare diseases must be established. The NIH Office of Rare Diseases should play a coordinating role. The genetics subcommittee of CLIAC should examine means of assuring the quality of laboratories performing tests for rare diseases.

These and the many other principles and recommendations of the Task

Force presented herein will help assure that genetic testing will be provided safely and effectively and that tests for rare diseases will be more widely available but used appropriately. The Task Force concludes that with implementation of these recommendations, genetic testing will continue to flourish.

NIH-HHS Working Group on Ethical, Legal, and Social Implications of Human Genome Research, May 19, 1997.

Document 20: "Orphan" Genetic Tests

Scientists know that hundreds of diseases have genetic causes, and with the growing knowledge of human genetics, it is becoming more possible to discover these causes and sometimes a cure. Many genetic diseases, however, while tragic, affect only a very small number of people. Doing the research to find causes and cures is extremely costly. As a result, research for some rare diseases is not being done. The author of the following article discusses the sorry decrease in some types of medical research.

When researchers cloned the gene for the rare ataxia-telangiectasia syndrome in June 1995, Brad Margus, founder of the Florida-based A-T Children's Project said he fully expected that a genetic test for this deadly disorder was just around the corner.

Two years later, Margus is still waiting. He said the research laboratories involved in the A-T gene hunt never intended to provide commercial testing. Many already have moved on to study the molecular biology of A-T, and others simply are not equipped to provide the service.

Margus said the problem is that no biotechnology companies have stepped forward to fill the testing void. The companies state, that for primarily financial reasons, they will not commit to commercializing tests for a small-market syndrome that affects maybe 500 Americans. They have to focus on the more common gene tests, such as the BRCA1 test, to compete in the marketplace.

These factors have left Margus and his fellow A-T families hanging in limbo, cut off from a potentially major diagnostic advance. "We know families that have two kids with A-T," said Margus. "They want a child who's healthy, one who's going to live. They ask if it's possible to get tested? I say, 'It can be done—but I can't get it done for you.'"

Neglected Diseases

As researchers discover more genes involved in rare diseases—usually considered to be conditions with a prevalence of fewer than 200,000 Americans—Margus' plight is becoming more common. According to several experts, genetic testing for rare diseases now faces the same problem that held back new drugs from the marketplace prior to the Orphan Drug Act of 1983. They are scientifically possible, but commercially unviable.

"When a gene for a rare disease is isolated, there is a lot of fanfare— appropriately so," said Les Biesecker, M.D., a scientist at the National

Human Genome Research Institute. "But when testing does not become a reality, the families begin to wonder, 'What was in this for us?'—also appropriately so. They want to know what's going on."

With no commercial testing available, some families are approaching the small research laboratories that study their disease in hopes of receiving a genetic test. The researchers say they feel a strong obligation to help the families. If their laboratories do not perform the tests, then who will?

But many of these scientists also wonder whether it is appropriate for researchers to fill that need. Nearly all research laboratories do not qualify as clinical laboratories because they lack certification under the Clinical Laboratory Improvement Act (CLIA) and by law must not report the results of their tests—no matter how informative—to patients, their families, or their doctors to help them make clinical decisions.

Most research laboratories would also have to siphon money from their research grants to do the test on the side, a misuse of their grant funds. Many do not have access to other needed resources, such as genetic counseling.

One fix would be the Orphan Drug Act. But Abbey Meyers, executive director of the National Organization for Rare Diseases, noted that the act covers drugs and biologics, but says nothing about genetic tests or devices.

Too Experimental

Some experts argue that this omission might just be a good thing. They say gene tests still are too experimental scientifically to be lumped in with promising drugs that have passed through Phase III clinical trials.

For example, scientists note that disease genes often are filled with missense mutations that cause amino acid substitutions in the gene's protein. Most of these changes have no biological effect. Yet, without adequate mutation screening and characterization, it is impossible to know which ones really matter, meaning false positives would be common.

They also say that most rare diseases, of which there are more than 5,000, are unknown commodities to most companies. Doctors are needed who have expertise in a rare condition to assist in the diagnosis. But finding these doctors can be a little like trying to find Waldo. In some cases, only two or maybe three groups worldwide specialize in a rare condition, making collaboration difficult.

According to some scientists, before laws are amended, something more basic needs to happen—the scientific community first needs to recognize that there are orphaned genetic tests out there. "We have to acknowledge that this is a problem" said Biesecker. "We have to decide, number one, if we are willing to solve it, and number two, how will we solve it?"

One possibility is for research laboratories with expertise in a rare disease to acquire CLIA approval. The potential upside is CLIA regulations, which require labs to meet a series of quality control standards, would force research laboratories to more rigorously validate and standardize their testing procedures. This would, in theory, ensure patients that they are receiving high-quality genetic information on which to base their clinical decisions.

But the idea already has been met with grumbles from some research scientists. They say their labs now function fine, and CLIA regulations are just one more case of the federal bureaucracy looking over their shoulders.

National Centers

Alternatively, Biesecker has suggested that a national or series of regional centers could be established for genetic testing of rare diseases. In an article published last year in the *Cambridge Quarterly of Healthcare Ethics*, Biesecker wrote, "This laboratory could be public or private, and could be a single or distributed entity. It would be staffed by a critical mass of molecular biologists, clinical consultants, and technical staff who would provide interaction, collaboration and critical evaluation of a variety of tests."

However, the idea might not ever leave the gate. Last September, a national Task Force on Genetic Testing wrote in its final report that it rejected the notion of a national center on the grounds that "assembling the necessary expertise for performing and interpreting all of the tests under one roof would be difficult or impossible."

But Biesecker and other scientists say they think there might be a middle ground. Research laboratories that study a rare disease could make linkages with nearby clinical laboratories. Bradley Popovich, Ph.D., director of the DNA Diagnostic Laboratory at the Oregon Health Sciences University in Portland, said his CLIA-approved clinical laboratory already has made such a link.

Popovich said his laboratory now performs among its many services linkage analysis—testing DNA for sequence markers linked to a disease—for families with a history of the rare ectodermal dysplasia. Although the test falls into the category of money loser, Popovich said it makes sense from a public health standpoint because Oregon Health Sciences University is home to one of the world's top research groups on ectodermal dysplasia.

He said his laboratory's link to the research group also has proven to be extremely efficient. When families contact the research group, it now can simply pass the request onward to Popovich's group. No longer do the scientists need to pine about the ethics of performing the service in the research laboratory.

Popovich also reiterates that testing for little-known rare diseases requires a team approach. "Linkage testing is only as good as the diagnosis of the key person," noted Popovich. "If I go back to my world-class researcher and say, 'Wait a minute, I'm really puzzled by this patient,' then I can resolve it. Without that world-class knowledge base, big mistakes can happen. You're basically trying to interpret in a vacuum."

All or Nothing

Popovich said it's important to recognize that genetic testing for rare diseases shouldn't be viewed by laboratories as an all-or-nothing proposition. "If I were doing only rare diseases, I'd be out of business because my institution wouldn't allow us to go that way," said Popovich. "Essentially, the agreement is we won't lose money, but we won't necessarily make a lot of money either. There's a balance here. We have some tests that pay their way and even put a little into the kitty. They help to pay for the money losers."

To help solve the problem of orphan genetic tests, Popovich said a national meeting might be needed to build consensus among the scientific community. He and others add that to ignore the problem will only make matters worse down the road when more genes for rare diseases enter the medical literature.

Without changes, as Biesecker wrote last year in the *Cambridge Quarterly*, rare diseases will continue to "exist in the shadows of the biotechnology revolution."

Bob Kuska, "Genetic Tests for Many Rare Diseases Headed for Orphan Status," *Journal of the National Cancer Institute*, December 3, 1997.

Document 21: Early Vision of Biomedical Future

It is only in the past several years that scientists have been able to do the kind of genetic engineering that has the potential to "build" human beings to have desired traits— or to be free of undesirable ones. Nevertheless, people have pondered the possibilities of this kind of science for many years. The following excerpt, first published in 1964, shows the kind of speculations common at that time.

If space-age biology continues along its present course, those Bug-Eyed-Monsters which used to slaver and glare from the covers of science fiction magazines may prove to be watered down versions of actual fact . . . trouble is—these BEMs could be *us*!

Such, at least, seems to be the sober, dedicated ambition of an entirely new breed of American scientist—the molecular biologists.

They've penetrated the atom of life itself and have nearly deciphered the secret of genetics—the code which has lain dormant in every cell of your body since conception—and which may be traced from all life forms now in existence back to its single common origin—that is, if the theory of all life having a common physical origin is true.

Today's molecular biologists have peered within the walls of living cells, studied the nuclei and made the most remarkable discovery in this history of science—existence of DNA and RNA, the basic building material of every form of life, insect, tree, fish, fowl or man. . . .

Both beneficial and detrimental viruses now can be manufactured synthetically. Theoretically, these synthetic viruses can be introduced into an artificially fertilized human egg. Some of the more far-out researchers already are talking about planting this egg in a nutrient solution, thus bypassing the human reproductive system almost entirely. They will be able to control heredity by learning all the molecular code signals of DNA and RNA. The entire field at this moment is being explored with great impatience, imagination, and little if any restraint. Scientists like Dr. Marshall Nirenberg, of the National Institute of Health, have learned the alphabet of the molecular language—all the letters of the code words for all 20 amino acids, for example. But Dr. Nirenberg says, "We must now learn to *spell* with the genetic code. *Only then can we hope to write messages of our own.*"

Philosophers, physicians and mystics always have been aware of the miraculous nature of the physical life we take so much for granted. Edgar Cayce, the great medical clairvoyant of Virginia Beach, said "there is intelligence in every cell of the body."

Each molecule of our body contains exactly the same coded information that was found in the fertilized egg; this information is repeated endlessly throughout the body. But it is highly selective. No one understands how the DNA in a brain cell knows enough to ignore the countless coded instructions for the functioning of cells in every other organ of the body except those necessary to keep the brain functioning properly, but it does. Whether it is found in a bone or in skin tissue, a muscle or the pituitary gland, DNA builds *only* the kind of cell that can be used by the organ it occupies, yet it is *capable* of building any other kind of cell.

This poses the same question presented by any kind of seed, the acorn for example. How does the acorn "know" it is supposed to form itself into an oak tree? A partial answer is the hereditary chain of DNA, which contains the Master Builder's instructions. Beyond this, we just don't know.

Infinitesimally tiny electrical charges emitted by the atoms and molecules may play an intimate part in the transmission of the coded instructions, but this hypothesis is now merely a remote fringe of scientific awareness.

We do know that any change made in the RNA in the nerve cells remains permanent. In the process of learning, RNA molecules are altered; when they divide this altered pattern is also divided and billions of "stencil-copies" of the original RNA remain as long as the organism continues to function. This has been crucially tested.

RNA, therefore, is the stuff memory is made of. Deterioration of mental and physical abilities due to what we call the aging process seems directly traceable to the molecules of the nucleic acids. Here's how it happens:

We are conceived and born with a perfectly "programmed" set of heredity factors; each and every atom fulfills its instructions for the formation of the body and the function and interaction of all its parts. During the first few months of life, many kinds of energy particles such as neutrinos from the Sun, beta and gamma rays from the distant stars, pass through our bodies. Occasionally one of them will interact with an atom of DNA and a tiny, virtually unnoticed change will take place inside the cell within an organ. This change indirectly affects the entire body. As the cells divide and are replaced, these minute alterations are carried forward in new generations of cells.

Being subjected to myriad energy particle impacts in the course of years, tiny changes accumulate and the original genetic message becomes scrambled in transmission and a progressively less efficient organism results. Cosmic particle impact also impairs the function of nerve cells in the brain that control memory, so faulty memory is one of the noticeable effects.

The foundation of a house can be attacked by termites over a period of years and the extent of the erosion may or may not be visible. But if termites go unchecked the house must eventually fall. This is analogous to life's eventual surrender to years of unceasing cosmic particle impact on the atoms of DNA. For all we know this could be what Nature has devised to keep matter and energy in a perpetual cycle of birth and dissolution. . . .

All the foregoing brings us to a very real possibility. When the genetic code is mastered and science is able to "write" out any desired genetic message, it will be put to practical use.

For instance, "writing out" the desired genetic code that will enable Homo sapiens to extract oxygen from water, the molecular biologists will have created Homo Aqueus—a true Fish-Man. Porpoises, whales and other aquatic mammals will be closer relatives to man than Homo Aqueus. At least they are warm-blooded *air* breathers,

There has been speculation among the space medicine experts about the kind of astronaut best suited to survive in the bitterly cold, rarefied atmosphere of Mars. The training of Peruvian Indians or Tibetan tribesmen, accustomed to living under similar conditions in the Andes or high Himalayas, has been postulated. But science already has by-passed the physiological ideas of the early space medics. By the time we have ships capable of landing on Mars, Venus and the moons of Jupiter, we probably will have developed special breeds of "men" with body chemistry programmed to adapt to any conceivable planetary environment.

Imagine the sort of creature it would take to live permanently in the unthinkable conditions on Jupiter. First of all, a crushing gravity more than 400 times that of Earth would make the existence of erect bipeds impossible. Man would have to revert to something like a fourlegged gorilla stance. In addition, he'd have to possess immense strength for locomotion under this crushing gravity. This means greatly increased size— and the creature would need a metabolism capable of thriving on what we consider noxious, deadly fumes: methane, ammonia, and probably hydrocarbons. Food—fuel for this strange metabolism is still another problem.

If this creature has blood at all, it will have to be a kind of permanent anti-freeze because the temperatures beneath that raging, crushing atmosphere make terrestrial polar regions seem like a tropical paradise. It is so dark that normal sight would be virtually useless; photons from the Sun simply cannot penetrate Jupiter's 18,000 mile-thick atmosphere of perpetually roaring, poisonous gases.

There is no doubt that molecular biology is capable of breeding new strains of man, probably even a creature capable of existing on Jupiter, Neptune or Uranus. But there is considerable doubt that this creature, even though its intelligence remained intact, would still be human. . . .

We've managed to develop thorobred horses and pedigreed canines and felines and to grow improved strains of plants, flowers and vegetables. Now we're on the brink of producing true super-men.

Our record for harmonious coexistence is sharply variant to the ideals for which we aim. What assurance is there that with imminent population control, a tyranny of genetics will not replace all known forms of government?

Once the full significance of large scale genetic manipulation dawns on ambitious bureaucrats or zealous humanitarians with political power, we may be faced with the greatest tyranny ever known to man—the creation by genetic alteration of a pre-programmed breed of human being whose only wish will be to work in beehive or ant-hill harmony and to selflessly serve the state.

Of course, he'll be very happy to do so because any form of dissatisfaction or even questioning will have been bred out of his psychology. Antisocial behavior will be impossible, thereby eliminating the need for police forces and armies. Creativity, scientific curiosity and artistic progress will go by the board, naturally. But this will be a small price to pay for blissful, uneventful existence. There'll be no need for advertising or propaganda. News will be a thing of the past because our interests will have been prearranged and nothing else will matter except our specified groove which we'll all attend to with robot-like precision.

This is one possible outcome of genetic manipulation. . . .

Whether we create Homo Superior, Homo Aqueus, or Homo Jovus, we might literally be creating the Frankenstein monsters of the future.

A long period of intensive, widely-publicized study should be demanded before the molecular biologists are given *carte blanche* to create any *un*human race of the future.

But who is doing anything about it?

Who even knows it's happening?

Joseph F. Goodavage, "Non-Men of the Future," *FATE Magazine*, October 1964. Reprinted with permission.

Document 22: Cloning: A History

The development of cloning has taken place over five decades. Here are highlights of that struggle.

Cloning's success didn't come out of the blue. Here is how nearly six decades of trial and error elapsed before one scientist got it right.

1938   A German embryologist theorizes that animals could be cloned by fusing an embryo with an egg cell.

1952   Two scientists try cloning frogs, without success.

1970   A British scientist repeats the frog experiment. He transplants frog embryo cells into egg cells. The eggs develop into tadpoles, but then die.

1981   Two scientists report that they've cloned mice from mouse embryo cells.

1982   No one can repeat the mouse experiment. The cloned mice turn out to be fake.

1984   A Danish embryologist clones sheep from early-stage embryo cells. Others later repeat his experiment using cattle, pigs, goats, rabbits, and monkeys.

1994   A scientist at the University of Wisconsin clones calves from late-stage embryo cells.

1996   In Scotland, scientists Ian Wilmut repeats the cow embryo experiment with sheep. He puts the embryo cells to "sleep" by starving them of nutrients. Then he fuses them with egg cells. The cells "wake up" and begin to divide like new embryo cells.

1997   Wilmut reports using the "sleeping cell" technique to clone a baby lamb named Dolly from an adult sheep's udder cell.

Chana Freiman Stiefel, "Cloning: Good Science or Baaad Idea?" *Science World*, May 2, 1997. Copyright © 1997 by Scholastic Inc. Reprinted by permission of Scholastic Inc.

Document 23: Recommendations

In June 1997, the National Bioethics Advisory Commission recommended that the cloning of human beings be banned. The following is an excerpt from their report.

I. The Commission concludes that at this time it is morally unacceptable for anyone in the public or private sector, whether in a research or clinical setting, to attempt to create a child using somatic cell nuclear transfer cloning. We have reached a consensus on this point because current scientific information indicates that this technique is not safe to use in humans at this time. Indeed, we believe it would violate important ethical obligations were clinicians or researchers to attempt to create a child using these particular technologies, which are likely to involve unacceptable risks to the fetus and/or potential child. Moreover, in addition to safety concerns, many other serious ethical concerns have been identified, which require much more widespread and careful public deliberation before this technology may be used.

The Commission, therefore, recommends the following for immediate action:

- A continuation of the current moratorium on the use of federal funding in support of any attempt to create a child by somatic cell nuclear transfer.

- An immediate request to all firms, clinicians, investigators, and professional societies in the private and non-federally funded sectors to comply voluntarily with the intent of the federal moratorium. Professional and scientific societies should make clear that any attempt to create a child by somatic cell nuclear transfer and implantation into a woman's body would at this time be an irresponsible, unethical, and unprofessional act.

II. The Commission further recommends that:

- Federal legislation should be enacted to prohibit anyone from attempting, whether in a research or clinical setting, to create a child through somatic cell nuclear transfer cloning. It is critical, however, that such legislation include a sunset clause to ensure that Congress will review the issue after a specified time period (three to five years) in order to decide whether the prohibition continues to be needed. If state legislation is enacted, it should also contain such a sunset provision. Any such legislation or associated regulation also ought to require that at some point prior to the expiration of the sunset period, an appropriate oversight body will evaluate and report on the current status of somatic cell nuclear transfer technology and on the ethical and social issues that its potential use to create human beings would raise in light of public understandings at that time.

III. The Commission also concludes that:

- Any regulatory or legislative actions undertaken to effect the foregoing prohibition on creating a child by somatic cell nuclear transfer should be carefully written so as not to interfere with other important areas of scientific research. In particular, no new regulations are required regarding the cloning of human DNA sequences and cell lines, since neither activity raises the scientific and ethical issues that arise from the attempt to create children through somatic cell nuclear transfer, and these fields of research have already provided important scientific and biomedical advances. Likewise, research on cloning animals by somatic cell nuclear transfer does not raise the issues implicated in attempting to use this technique for human cloning, and its continuation should only be subject to existing regulations regarding the humane use of animals and review by institution-based animal protection committees.

- If a legislative ban is not enacted, or if a legislative ban is ever lifted, clinical use of somatic cell nuclear transfer techniques to create a child should be preceded by research trials that are governed by the twin protections of independent review and informed consent, consistent with existing norms of human subjects protection.

- The United States Government should cooperate with other nations and international organizations to enforce any common aspects of their respective policies on the cloning of human beings.

IV. The Commission also concludes that different ethical and religious perspectives and traditions are divided on many of the important moral issues that surround any attempt to create a child using somatic cell nuclear transfer techniques. Therefore, we recommend that:

- The federal government, and all interested and concerned parties, encourage widespread and continuing deliberation on these issues in order to further our understanding of the ethical and social implications of this technology and to enable society to produce appropriate long-term policies regarding this technology should the time come when present concerns about safety have been addressed.

V. Finally, because scientific knowledge is essential formal citizens to participate in a full and informed fashion in the governance of our complex society, the Commission recommends that:

- Federal departments and agencies concerned with science should cooperate in seeking out and supporting opportunities to provide information and education to the public in the area of genetics, and on other developments in the biomedical sciences, especially where these affect important cultural practices, values, and beliefs.

National Bioethics Advisory Commission, "Cloning Human Beings: Report and Recommendations," June 1997.

Document 24: Respect for Nature and God

Among the strongest voices speaking against cloning are those of the religious community. Many people with strong religious beliefs feel that cloning is putting into human hands a power that should belong to God alone—that of creating human beings. Stephen G. Post, associate professor of bioethics at the Center for Biomedical Ethics at Case Western University in Cleveland, Ohio, wrote a powerful treatise arguing against cloning from a religious perspective. Here is an excerpt.

In the words of Jewish bioethicist Fred Rosner, cloning goes so far in violating the structure of nature that it can be considered as "encroaching on the Creator's domain." Is the union of sex, marriage, love and procreation something to dismiss lightly?

Marriage is the union of female and male that alone allows for procreation in which children can benefit developmentally from both a mother and father. In the Gospel of Mark, Jesus draws on ancient Jewish teachings when he asserts, "Therefore what God has joined together, let no man separate." Regardless of the degree of extendedness in any family, there remains the core nucleus: wife, husband and children. Yet the nucleus can be split by various cultural forces (e.g., infidelity as interesting, illegitimacy as chic), poverty, patriarchal violence and now cloning.

A cursory study of the Hebrew Bible shows the exuberant and immensely powerful statements of Genesis 1, in which a purposeful, ordering God pronounces that all stages of creation are "good." The text proclaims, "So God created humankind in his image, in the image of God he created them, male and female he created them" (Gen. 1:27). This God commands the couple, each equally in God's likeness, to "be fruitful and multiply." The divine prototype was thus established at the very outset of the Hebrew Bible: "Therefore a man leaves his father and his mother and clings to his wife, and they become one flesh" (Gen. 2:24).

The dominant theme of Genesis 1 is creative intention. God creates, and what is created procreates, thereby ensuring the continued presence of God's creation. The creation of man and woman is good in part because it will endure. Catholic natural law ethicists and Protestant proponents of "orders of creation" alike find divine will and principle in the passages of Genesis 1.

A major study on the family by the Christian ethicist Max Stackhouse suggests that just as the pre-Socratic philosophers discovered still valid truths about geometry, so the biblical authors of Chapters One and Two of Genesis "saw something of the basic design, purpose, and context of life that transcends every sociohistorical epoch." Specifically, this design includes "fidelity in communion" between male and female oriented toward "generativity" and an enduring family the precise social details of which are worked out in the context of political economies. . . .

Christians side with the deep wisdom of the teachings of Jesus, manifest in a thoughtful respect for the laws of nature that reflect the word of God. Christians simply cannot and must not underestimate the threat of human cloning to unravel what is both naturally and eternally good.

Stephen G. Post, "The Judeo-Christian Case Against Cloning," *America*, June 21, 1997.

STUDY QUESTIONS

Chapter 1

1. What are some examples of medical achievements that have been gained through the use of animals in research?

2. Give examples of medical failures despite the use of animals in research.

3. What are some alternatives to using animals in research?

4. Why are humans sometimes used in medical research?

5. What is a clinical trial, and what part does it play in medical research?

6. What are some of the measures that have been taken to protect humans used in medical research?

Chapter 2

1. What is the main reason people donate organs?

2. Describe four ways that might promote more organ donation.

3. What are the main objections to allowing human organs to be bought and sold?

4. What is informed consent? Do you think requiring informed consent helps or hinders the organ donation program?

Chapter 3

1. What are two practical ways genetic testing can be harmful for an individual?

2. Why might it be harmful for a person to discover that he or she does *not* carry a lethal gene.

3. Why might it be helpful for a person to discover that he or she *does* carry a lethal gene?

4. Explain why it is difficult to keep information gained in genetic testing private.

5. How might gene therapy be used to improve a person's health?

6. Give some examples of successful gene therapy.

7. Name the factors suggesting that gene therapy will not end disease.

Chapter 4

1. What are the main arguments against cloning humans?

2. In what ways might a clone differ from its original source?

3. Name three benefits of cloning humans.

4. Explain why you think cloning a whole basketball team of Michael Jordans would be a good or bad idea.

ORGANIZATIONS TO CONTACT

The editors have compiled the following list of organizations concerned with the issues debated in this book. The descriptions are derived from materials provided by the organizations. All have publications or information available for interested readers. The list was compiled on the date of publication of the present volume; the information provided here may change. Be aware that many organizations take several weeks or longer to respond to inquiries, so allow as much time as possible.

Ag Bioethics Forum
c/o Professor Gary Comstock, Bioethics Program Coordinator
402 Catt Hall, Iowa State University
Ames, IA 50011-1306
(515) 294-0054 • e-mail: comstock@iastate.edu
website: http://www.grad-college.iastate.edu/bioethics
The forum examines bioethical issues concerning agriculture, food, animals, and the environment. It publishes *Ag Bioethics Forum*, a biannual newsletter that explores the ethical dilemmas that arise when genetic engineering is applied to agriculture.

American Anti-Vivisection Society
801 Old York Rd., Suite 204
Jenkintown, PA 19046-1685
(215) 887-0816 • fax: (215) 887-2088
e-mail: aavsonline@aol.com
website: http://www.aavs.org
The oldest animal rights group in America, the society opposes all animal experimentation. It publishes educational pamphlets and the quarterly *AV* magazine.

American Civil Liberties Union (ACLU)
125 Broad St., 18th Fl.
New York, NY 10004-2400
(212) 549-2500 • publications: (800) 775-ACLU (2258)
e-mail: aclu@aclu.org
website: http://www.aclu.org
The ACLU champions the civil rights provided by the U.S.

Constitution. The union is concerned that genetic testing may lead to genetic discrimination in the workplace, including the refusal to hire and the termination of employees who are at risk for developing genetic conditions. The ACLU publishes a variety of handbooks, pamphlets, reports, and newsletters, including the quarterly *Civil Liberties* and the monthly *Civil Liberties Alert*.

American Medical Association (AMA)
515 N. State St.
Chicago, IL 60610
(312) 464-5000
website: http://www.ama-assn.org
The AMA is the largest professional association for medical doctors. It helps set standards for medical education and practices, and it is a powerful lobby in Washington for physicians' interests. The association publishes journals for many medical fields, including the monthly *Archives of Surgery* and the weekly *JAMA*.

American Society of Law, Medicine, and Ethics (ASLME)
765 Commonwealth Ave., 16th Fl.
Boston, MA 02215
(617) 262-4990 • fax: (617) 437-7596
e-mail: aslme@bu.edu
website: http://www.aslme.org
The society's members include physicians, attorneys, health care administrators, and others interested in the relationship between law, medicine, and ethics. It takes no positions but acts as a forum for discussion of issues such as genetic engineering. The organization has an information clearinghouse and a library. It publishes the quarterlies *American Journal of Law & Medicine* and the *Journal of Law, Medicine & Ethics*; the periodic *ASLME Briefings*; and various books.

BC Biotechnology Alliance (BCBA)
1122 Mainland St., #450
Vancouver, BC V6B 5L1, CANADA
(604) 689-5602 • fax: (604) 689-4198
website: http://www.biotech.bc.ca
The BCBA is an association for producers and users of biotechnology. The alliance works to increase public awareness and understanding of biotechnology, including the awareness of its potential contributions to society. The alliance's publications include the bimonthly newsletter *Biofax* and the annual magazine *Biotechnology in BC*.

Biotechnology Industry Organization (BIO)
1625 K St. NW, #1100
Washington, DC 20006
(202) 857-0244 • fax: (202) 857-0237
e-mail: info@bio.org
website: http://www.bio.org

BIO is composed of companies engaged in industrial biotechnology. It monitors government actions that affect biotechnology and promotes increased public understanding of biotechnology through its educational activities and workshops. BIO is committed to the socially responsible use of biotechnology to save or improve lives, improve the quality and abundance of food, and clean up hazardous waste. It publishes on-line bulletins and the bimonthly newsletter *BIO News*.

Childbirth By Choice Trust
344 Bloor St. West, #306
Toronto, ON M5S 3A7, CANADA
(416) 961-7812 • fax: (416) 961-3473
e-mail: cbtrust@idirect.com
website: http://web.idirect.com/~cbctrust

The trust aims to educate the public on fertility control issues, such as contraceptive use, abortion, and unintended pregnancy. It hopes to make all options available to women who are unhappily pregnant, including abortion, childbirth, and adoption. The trust provides educational pamphlets that provide information about fertility control issues, such as *Abortion: The Medical Procedure, Contraceptive Use in Canada*, and *Economics of Unintended Pregnancy*. These pamphlets can be ordered through their website or by mail.

Council for Responsible Genetics
5 Upland Rd., Suite 3
Cambridge, MA 02140
(617) 868-0870 • fax: (617) 491-5344
e-mail: crg@essential.org
website: http://www.essential.org/crg

The council is a national organization of scientists, health professionals, trade unionists, women's health activists, and others who work to ensure that biotechnology is developed safely and in the public interest. The council publishes the bimonthly newsletter *GeneWatch* and position papers on the Human Genome Project, genetic discrimination, germ-line modifications, and DNA-based identification systems.

Foundation for Biomedical Research
818 Connecticut Ave. NW, Suite 303
Washington, DC 20006
(202) 457-0654 • fax: (202) 457-0659
e-mail: info@fbresearch.org
website: http://www.fbresearch.org

The foundation supports humane animal research and serves to inform and educate the public about the necessity and importance of laboratory animals in biomedical research and testing. It publishes a bimonthly newsletter, videos, films, and numerous background papers, including *The Use of Animals in Biomedical Research and Testing* and *Caring for Laboratory Animals.*

The Hastings Center
Garrison, NY 10524-5555
(914) 424-4040 • fax: (914) 424-4545
e-mail: mail@thehastingscenter.org

Since its founding in 1969, the center has played a central role in responding to advances in medicine, the biological sciences, and the social sciences by raising ethical questions related to such advances. It conducts research on ethical issues and provides consultations. The center publishes books, papers, guidelines, and the bimonthly *Hastings Center Report.*

Living Bank
PO Box 6725
Houston, TX 77265
(713) 528-2971 • fax: (713) 961-0979 • hot line: (800) 528-2971
e-mail: jeiche@livingbank.org
website: http://www.livingbank.org

The bank is an international registry and referral service for people wishing to donate organs and/or tissue for transplantation, therapy, or research. Its volunteers speak to civic organizations about the benefits of organ donation, and its 350,000 donor population spreads through fifty states and sixty-three foreign countries. It provides educational materials on organ donation and publishes a bimonthly newsletter, the *Living Banker.*

People for the Ethical Treatment of Animals (PETA)
501 Front St.
Norfolk, VA 23510

(757) 622-PETA (7382) • fax: (757) 622-0457
website: http://www.peta-online.org
PETA is an educational, activist group that opposes all forms of animal exploitation. It conducts rallies and demonstrations to focus attention on animal experimentation, the fur fashion industry, and the killing of animals for human consumption—three issues it considers institutionalized cruelty. Through the use of films, slides, and pictures, PETA hopes to educate the public about human chauvinist attitudes toward animals and about the conditions in slaughterhouses and research laboratories. It publishes reports on animal experimentation and animal farming and the periodic *People for the Ethical Treatment of Animals—Action Alerts*.

United Network for Organ Sharing (UNOS)
1100 Boulders Pkwy., Suite 500
Richmond, VA 23225
(804) 330-8500 • fax: (804) 330-8507
website: http://www.unos.org
UNOS is a system of transplant and organ procurement centers, tissue-typing labs, and transplant surgical teams. It was formed to match organ donors with people in need of organs. By law, organs used for transplants must be cleared through UNOS. The network also formulates and implements national policies on equal access to organs and organ allocation, organ procurement, and AIDS testing. It publishes the quarterly *UNOS Update*.

FOR FURTHER READING

Books

B.D. Colen, *Hard Choices: Mixed Blessings of Modern Medical Technology.* New York: G.P. Putnam's Sons, 1986. Many case histories illustrate the dilemmas physicians face as a result of advances in technology. These include issues of reproductive rights, organ replacement, genetic manipulation, and death.

Jeffrey Finn and Eliot L. Marshall, *Medical Ethics.* New York: Chelsea House, 1990. Examines several of the key issues related to biomedical advances, including reproduction, allocation of resources, and choosing death.

Pat Stave Helmberger, *Transplants: Unwrapping the Second Gift of Life.* Minneapolis: Chronimed, 1992. Interviews with organ recipients and their families explore the physical, psychological, and ethical impact of transplants on all concerned.

Margaret O. Hyde and Elizabeth H. Forsyth, M.D., *Medical Dilemmas.* New York: G.P. Putnam's Sons, 1990. An overview of several of the crucial issues in medical ethics and technology, including animal use in research, gene therapy, organ transplantation, and dilemmas surrounding AIDS.

Daniel Jussim, *Medical Ethics: Moral and Legal Conflicts in Health Care.* New York: Julian Messner, 1991. Overview of significant issues of life and death illustrated by numerous case histories.

Margot C.J. Mabie, *Bioethics and the New Medical Technology.* New York: Atheneum, 1993. Overview of several of the troubling questions raised by advances in medical technology. Includes discussion of reproductive technology, allocation of resources, and ending life.

Lawrence Pringle, *The Animal Rights Controversy.* San Diego: Harcourt Brace Jovanovich, 1989. Discussion of the issues involved in the use of animals in research.

Tamara L. Roleff, ed., *Biomedical Ethics.* San Diego: Greenhaven Press, 1998. An excellent collection of articles giving pros and cons on topics such as cloning, genetic technology, research ethics, and reproductive technology.

Victoria Sherrow, *Bioethics and the High-Tech Medicine.* New York: Twenty-First Century Books, 1996. An easy-to-understand look at genetic technology, research ethics, organ transplants, prolonging life, and other biomedical issues.

Lisa Yount, *Issues in Biomedical Ethics.* San Diego: Lucent Books, 1997. A discussion of the pros and cons of six major issues in the area of biomedical ethics: the slippery slope, the allocation of health resources, physician-assisted death, the use of animals in medical research, genetic testing, and setting limits in biomedical decision making. Illustrations and appendixes enhance the text.

Periodicals

General

Discover, several articles exploring the new technology and how it affects biomedical issues, May 1998.

Medical Research

"Battle over Animal Rights," *Current Events*, December 9, 1996.

Ken Flieger, "Testing Drugs in People," U.S. Food and Drug Administration. On-line. Internet. Available at: http://www.fda.gov/fdac/special/newdrug/testing.html.

Leslie Ann Horvitz, "Are Animal Advocates Biting the Hand of Dedicated Docs?" *Insight on the News*, May 19, 1997.

Richard McCourt, "Model Patients," *Discover*, August 1990.

Richard C. Thompson, "Protecting 'Human Guinea Pigs,'" U.S. Food and Drug Administration. On-line. Internet. Available at http://www.fda.gov/fdac/special/newdrug/guinea.html.

Organ Transplants

Claudia Glenn Dowling, "Rondie's Gift," *Life*, March 1997.

Celeste Fremon, "'I Wanted to Live,'" *Good Housekeeping*, February 1997.

Jeanne Marie Laskas, "Angel of the Heart Ward," *Good Housekeeping*, November 1997.

"Selling Organs: Lifesaver or Death Sentence?" *Current Events*, November 14, 1997.

Cloning

Barry Came, "The Prospect of Evil," *Maclean's*, March 10, 1997.

"Cloning Isn't Sexy," *Commonweal*, March 28, 1997.

Christine Gorman, "Neti and Ditto: Two Cute New Clones Are Too

Close for Comfort," *Time*, March 17, 1997.

———, "To Ban or Not to Ban?" *Time*, June 16, 1997.

Charles Krauthammer, "Of Headless Mice . . . and Men: The Ultimate Cloning Horror," *Time*, January 12, 1998.

Jay Mader, "Bring 'em Back Alive," *U.S. News & World Report*, October 13, 1997.

Madeleine J. Nash, "The Age of Cloning," *Time*, March 10, 1997.

———, "The Case for Cloning," *Time*, February 9, 1998.

———, "Cloning's Kevorkian," *Time*, January 12, 1998.

Charles Pellegrino, "Resurrecting Dinosaurs," *Omni*, Fall 1995.

Larry Reibstein and Gregory Beals, "A Cloned Chop, Anyone?" *Newsweek*, March 10, 1997.

Robert Wright, "Can Souls Be Xeroxed?" *Time*, March 10, 1997.

Genetic Technology

David Brindley, "Case of Denial," *U.S. News & World Report*, June 30, 1997.

Shannon Brownlee, "How Do Genes Switch On?" *U.S. News & World Report*, August 25, 1997.

Jeff Goldberg, "A Head Full of Hope," *Discover*, April 1998.

Michael Kinsley, "Oh, My Aching Genes! Drawing a Tube of Blood Is Just One of the Many Ways We Unfairly Judge People," *Time*, September 29, 1997.

Jill Smolowe, "Seeing the Future," *Time*, Special Issue: Heroes of Medicine, Fall 1997.

WORKS CONSULTED

Books

Robert M. Arnold, M.D. et al., eds., *Procuring Organs for Transplant: The Debate over Non-Heart-Beating Cadaver Protocols.* Baltimore: Johns Hopkins University Press, 1995. Collection of professional articles relating to the definition of death, ethical sources of organs for transplant, and other related issues. Multiple points of view are represented.

Daniel Callahan, *The Troubled Dream of Life: Living with Mortality.* New York: Simon & Schuster, 1993. Examines the relationship between modern medicine and death, focusing on legal, ethical, and personal issues.

Arthur L. Caplan, *If I Were a Rich Man Could I Buy a Pancreas? And Other Essays on the Ethics of Healthcare.* Bloomington: Indiana University Press, 1992. Noted bioethicist ruminates on several aspects of biomedical technology.

Nancy Dubler, and David Nimmons, *Ethics on Call: A Medical Ethicist Shows How to Take Charge of Life-and-Death Choices.* New York: Harmony Books, 1992. Written for a general audience, this book is intended to empower patients and their families who, the authors feel, have "lost control over life-and-death decisions in our health-care system." They are particularly concerned about technology-related issues such as life extension, organ transplants, and keeping the decision-making power in the hands of people rather than the medical establishment.

Samuel Gorovitz, *Doctors' Dilemmas: Moral Conflict and Medical Care.* New York: Macmillan, 1982. Explores ethical issues physicians face daily, including allocation of scarce medical resources, efforts at achieving value-free medicine, organ transplants, and death.

Milton D. Heiftez, M.D., *Easier Said than Done: Moral Decisions in Medical Uncertainty.* Buffalo, NY: Prometheus Books, 1992. An experienced physician calls on his years of critical medical decision making and many case histories to propose controversial guidelines in response to medical ethical dilemmas.

Daniel J. Kevles, *In the Name of Eugenics: Genetics and the Uses of Human Heredity.* Cambridge: Harvard University Press, 1995. Examines the history of the eugenics movement and its successor, today's genetic engineering.

Jonathan Kwitny, *Acceptable Risks*. New York: Poseidan, 1992. Chronicles two gay men's efforts to gain experimental drugs for HIV and AIDS patients, contrary to FDA practice.

Stephen E. Lammers and Allen Verhey, eds., *On Moral Medicine: Theological Perspectives in Medical Ethics*. Grand Rapids, MI: William B. Eerdmans, 1987. College- or professional-level textbook/anthology containing more than one hundred articles examining many aspects of medical ethics. Of particular interest to readers of this book are chapters 12 ("Genetic Control"), 18 ("Research and Experimentation"), and 19 ("Allocation and Distribution").

Howard Levine, *Life Choices: Confronting the Life and Death Decisions Created by Modern Medicine*. New York: Simon & Schuster, 1986. Thoughtful guide to many of the critical health issues that face people today, including organ transplantation, genetic manipulation, deciding about death, and reproductive technology.

Jeff Lyon and Peter Gorner, *Altered Fates: Gene Therapy and the Retooling of Human Life*. New York: W.W. Norton, 1995. The story of the first efforts of gene therapy.

Ruth Macklin, *Mortal Choices: Bioethics in Today's World*. New York: Pantheon, 1987. Overview of the dilemmas of doctors and families when faced with life-and-death decisions affected by technology. How does one decide when to offer treatment and when to withhold it? Who should receive the benefits of technology and who should not? Is everything that is possible desirable?

Gina Maranto, *Quest for Perfection: The Drive to Breed Better Human Beings*. New York: Scribner, 1996. Examines the schemes for improving the human species throughout history, but concentrates on today's biomedical advances.

Thomas H. Murray, Mark A. Rothstein, and Robert F. Murray Jr., *The Human Genome Project and the Future of Health Care*. Bloomington: Indiana University Press, 1996. Essays exploring the benefits and dangers of learning more about the human genes.

Terry O'Neill, ed., *Biomedical Ethics: Opposing Viewpoints*. San Diego: Greenhaven Press, 1994. Anthology of articles debating the pros and cons of biomedical ethics, human- and animal-based medical research, organ transplantation, fetal tissue research, reproductive technology, and genetic research.

Michael J. Reiss and Roger Straugthan, *Improving Nature? The*

Science and Ethics of Genetic Engineering. Cambridge, England: Cambridge University Press, 1996. Discusses many of the essential issues revolving around genetic engineering.

Jeremy Rifkin, *The Biotech Century: Harnessing the Gene and Remaking the World.* New York: Tarcher/Putnam, 1998. Discusses the wide-ranging changes taking place in the world and in humanity itself as a result of biotechnological advances, and asks whether the advances are worth the cost.

Thomas Scully, M.D., and Celia Scully, *Playing God: The New World of Medical Choices.* New York: Simon & Schuster, 1987. A guide for patients and their families faced with difficult health care decisions, ranging from developing a positive relationship with the physician to organ transplants, dealing with terminal illnesses, and reproductive issues. Includes extensive appendix of useful documents including "A Patient's Bill of Rights," "Living Will and Durable Power of Attorney," and "Uniform Anatomical Gift Act."

Lee M. Silver, *Remaking Eden: Cloning and Beyond in the Brave New World.* New York: Avon, 1997. The social implications of human cloning.

Claire Sylvia and William Novak, *A Change of Heart: A Memoir.* New York: Warner, 1988. Woman receives heart transplant and believes she also received personality traits of the donor.

Paul A. Winters, ed., *Cloning.* San Diego: Greenhaven Press, 1997. A collection of articles covering many aspects of the issue of cloning, both pro and con.

Doris Teichler Zallan, *Does It Run in the Family? A Consumer's Guide to DNA Testing for Genetic Disorders.* New Brunswick, NJ: Rutgers University Press, 1977. Examines the pros and cons of genetic testing, with particular attention to families who are prone to inherited genetic disorders; includes list of resources for families considering genetic testing.

Periodicals

General

Peter Carlin, "Art Caplan: When Doctors Need an Ethics Check," *People Weekly,* November 3, 1997.

Carolyn M. Clancy and Howard Brody, "Managed Care: Jekyll or Hyde?" *JAMA,* January 25, 1995.

Yochi Dreazen, "Ethicists and Scientists Ask: What Will Follow

Cancer Cure?" Washington Bureau of the *St. Paul Pioneer Press*, June 16, 1998.

Ellen Goodman, "McCaughey Miracle Spawns Hard Questions," Washington Post Writers Group, December 7, 1997.

Mary Hager and Adam Rogers, "A Biotech Roadblock," *Newsweek*, April 13, 1998.

————, "Miracles That May Keep You Going," *Newsweek*, June 30, 1997.

"How We Heal," special section, *Newsweek Extra: 2000 A New Millennium*, Winter 1997–1998.

Maclean Hunter, "The Second Genesis: Science May Be Ready to Create a Perfect World—But Who Will Define Perfect?" *Maclean's*, May 4, 1998.

Tom Majeski, "Hale and Hearty," *St. Paul Pioneer Press*, December 30, 1997.

Michael Schachner, "Health Care Reform Requires Some Rationing, Says Expert," *Business Insurance*, April 25, 1994.

Medical Research

"AZT Trials in Developing Countries: What's Next?" *AIDS Alert*, February 1998.

Neal D. Barnard, "What Works for Animals Isn't Necessarily Good for Humans," Knight-Ridder/Tribune News Service, January 14, 1998.

Sue Berkman, "Volunteering for Medical Research," *Good House-keeping*, August 1991.

Jennifer Brookes, "Clinical Trials: How They Work, Why We Need Them," *Closing the Gap* (newsletter of the Office of Minority Health, U.S. Department of Health and Human Services), December 1997–January 1998.

————, "Minority Participation in Clinical Trials," *Closing the Gap* (newsletter of the Office of Minority Health, U.S. Department of Health and Human Services), December 1997–January 1998.

Michael D'Antonio, "Atomic Guinea Pigs," *New York Times Magazine*, August 31, 1997.

Michael Day, "Third-World Human Lab Rats," *New Scientist*, May 17, 1997.

"Don't Try This at Home," *People Weekly*, April 20, 1998.

John Gallagher, "A Vaccine at What Cost?" *Advocate*, November 25, 1997.

Christine Gorman, "None But the Brave," *Time*, October 6, 1997.

Daniel S. Greenberg, "Human Data and Abuse in Research Comes to Light in the USA," *Lancet*, October 11, 1997.

Charles W. Henderson, "Controversy: AIDS Vaccine Study Director's Actions Questioned," *AIDS Weekly Plus*, February 16, 1998.

———, "Patients Seek Use of Experimental Antibody," *AIDS Weekly Plus*, January 19, 1998.

Michael P. Hutchens, "Grave Robbing and Ethics in the 19th Century," *JAMA*, October 1, 1997.

Anna Kohn, "So You Want to Be a Guinea Pig?" *Chatelaine*, December 1997.

Gina Kolata, "Rights vs. Research: Question of Ethics," New York Times News Service, April 1, 1998.

Wendy K. Mariner, "Public Confidence in Public Health Research Ethics," *Public Health Reports*, January/February 1997.

Charles Marwick, "Assessment of Exception to Informed Consent," *JAMA*, November 5, 1997.

———, "Improved Protection for Human Research Subjects," *JAMA*, February 4, 1998.

Edward Mbidde, "Bioethics and Local Circumstances," *Science*, January 9, 1998.

Jonathan D. Moreno, "The Dilemmas of Experimenting on People," *Technology Review*, July 1997.

Eugene Passamani, "Clinical Trials—Are They Ethical?" *New England Journal of Medicine*, vol. 324, no. 20, May 30, 1991.

"Research Unit Reports," *Guinea Pig Zero: A Journal for Human Pharmaceutical Research Subjects*, No. 2 (1997).

Pol Riis, "Ethics," *JAMA*, June 18, 1997.

Julian Savulescu, "Commentary: Safety of Participants in Non-Therapeutic Research Must Be Ensured," *British Medical Journal*, March 21, 1998.

Scientific American, February 1997, special section of four articles debating the benefits and pitfalls of using animals in medical research.

Dixie E. Snider Jr. and Donna F. Stroup, "Defining Research When It Comes to Public Health," *Public Health Reports*, January/February 1997.

Wendeline L. Wagner, "They Shoot Monkeys, Don't They?" *Harper's Magazine*, August 1997.

"What Are Clinical Trials About?" Office of Cancer Communications, National Cancer Institute, Bethesda, Maryland, 1996.

Organ Transplants

Colleen D. Anderson, "Organ Transplantation: Sources of Support for Patients and Caregivers—a Personal Journey," *RQ*, Spring 1996.

Ian Austen, "Stock Ticker," *Canadian Business*, September 26, 1997.

Stephen Baker, "Who Gets a Liver—and Who Doesn't?" *Business Week*, December 9, 1996.

Judith Yates Borger, "Heart: A Story of Loss and Life," seven-part series, *St. Paul Pioneer Press*. December 28, 1997–January 3, 1998, and follow-up letter, Susan Gunderson, "Heart Series Did Organ Donation a Regrettable Disservice," January 8, 1998.

Laurent Castellucci, "Organ Transplants Carry a Rare Risk of Hidden Cancers," *Journal of the National Cancer Institute*, March 4, 1998.

Ellen Goodman, "The Body as Commodity," Washington Post Writers Group, March 10, 1998.

"Liver Spats," *Economist*, January 25, 1997.

Merrill Matthews Jr., "Have a Heart, But Pay for It," *Insight on the News*, January 9, 1995.

Laura Meckler, "Agency Reverses Policy on Livers for Transplantation," Associated Press, February 27, 1998.

———, "Transplant Network Fights Feds over Organ Distribution System," Associated Press, May 30, 1998.

Patty Reiner, "Final Decisions," *Houston Chronicle*, November 27, 1997.

Catrien Ross, "Towards Acceptance of Organ Transplantation?" *Lancet*, August 17, 1996.

Leslie Brooks Suzukamo, "Local Transplant Officials Worry over New Policy's Implications," *St. Paul Pioneer Press*, March 27, 1998.

Robert M. Tenery Jr., "More Patients Need Their Second Chance at Life," *American Medical News*, April 10, 1995.

Genetic Technology

Anne L. Finger, "How Would You Handle These Ethical Dilemmas?" *Medical Economics*, October 27, 1997.

Mary Jane Fisher, "NAHU Takes Stand on Genetic Testing," *National Underwriter Life & Health*, Financial Services Edition, October 13, 1997.

Robert H. Gettlin, "Genetic Testing Takes Center Stage," *Best's Review*, Life-Health Insurance Edition, August 1997.

Diane M. Gianelli, "'Enhancement' Gene Therapy Raises a New Ethical Dilemma," *American Medical News*, October 6, 1997.

Eric S. Grace, "Better Health Through Gene Therapy," *Futurist*, January/February 1998.

Samuel Greengard, "Genetic Testing: Should You Be Afraid? It's No Joke," *Workforce*, July 1997.

Daniel Q. Haney, "Need a Bypass? Someday You Can Grow Your Own," Associated Press, November 10, 1997.

Neil A. Holtzman et al., "Predictive Genetic Testing: From Basic Research to Clinical Practice," *Science*, October 24, 1997.

"Hope and Fear," *American Medical News*, April 20, 1998.

"Human Genome Project Information," U.S. Department of Energy. On-line. Internet. Available at http://www.ornl.gov/TechResources/HumanGenome/home.html, June 21, 1998.

Susan Jenks, "Gene Therapy: A New Role in Disrupting Tumor's Blood Supply?" *Journal of the National Cancer Institute*, February 18, 1998.

Bob Kuska, "Genetic Tests for Many Rare Diseases Headed for Orphan Status," *Journal of the National Cancer Institute*, December 3, 1997.

Carolyn Lerman, "The Influence of Psychological Distress on Use of Genetic Testing for Cancer Risk," *JAMA*, November 26, 1997.

Greg Linde, "Getting Frenetic About Genetics," *Best's Review*, Life-Health Insurance Edition, August 1997.

Wendy C. McKinnon et al., "Predisposition Genetic Testing for Late-Onset Disorders in Adults: A Position Paper of the National Society of Genetic Counselors," *JAMA*, October 15, 1997.

Michelle Meadows, "Genetic Testing Can Lead to Fear of Stigmatization," *Closing the Gap*, December 1997/January 1998.

David L. Page et al., "Genetic Testing and Informed Consent," *JAMA*, September 10, 1997.

Bruce Ponder, "Genetic Testing for Cancer Risk," *Science*, November 7, 1997.

Rosamond Rhodes, "Genetic Links, Family Ties, and Social Bonds: Rights and Responsibilities in the Face of Genetic Knowledge," *Journal of Medicine and Philosophy*, February 1998.

Catherine Sack, "Tropic of Cancer," *New Republic*, June 2, 1997.

Caroline Saucer, "Do the Right Thing," *Best's Review*, Property-Casualty Insurance Edition, November 1997.

Paul Smaglik, "Gene Therapy—the Next Generation," *Scientist*, May 11, 1998.

David Stipp, "Gene Testing Starts to Pay Off: Medical Miracles," *Fortune*, August 4, 1997.

Helen Thorpe, "Cancer Patience," *Texas Monthly*, January 1997.

Kathleen Kennedy Townsend, "The Double-Edged Helix: Advances in Genetic Testing Reveal Yet Another Reason We Need National Health Insurance," *Washington Monthly*, November 1997.

Gretchen Vogel, "From Science Fiction to Ethics Quandary," *Science*, September 19, 1997.

"When Genetic Testing Might Be Appropriate: The Role of the Genetic Counselor," *Tufts University Health & Nutrition Letter*, March 1998.

Patricia J. Williams, "I a Child and Thou a Lamb," *Nation*, February 2, 1998.

Lyric Wallwork Winik, "When You Should Consider a Genetic Test," *Parade*, April 19, 1998.

Tim Wolter, "There Are Simply Some Things We Should Not Know," *American Medical News*, April 7, 1997.

Cloning

Rudy Baum, "Playing God," *Chemical & Engineering News*, March

24, 1997.

Jean Bethke Elshtain, "Bad Seed," *New Republic*, February 9, 1998.

———, "Ewegenics," *New Republic*, March 31, 1997.

———, "Our Bodies, Our Clones," *New Republic*, August 4, 1997.

"Fear of Cloning," *Economist*, January 17, 1998.

Rod Fee, "Well . . . Hello, Dolly!" *Successful Farming*, May/June 1997.

Alison Fitzgerald, "Cloned Calves Could Be Pharmaceutical Factories," Associated Press, January 21, 1998.

John Garvey, "The Mystery Remains: What Cloning Can't Reproduce," *Commonweal*, March 28, 1997.

Diane M. Gianelli, "Cloning Ban May Hinder Research," *American Medical News*, October 20, 1997.

———, "Presidential Panel Advocates Ban on Cloning," *American Medical News*, June 23, 1997.

Ellen Goodman, "Cloning Needs to Be Nipped Before It Buds," Washington Post Writers Group, February 17, 1998.

Cecil Johnson, "Cloning: Killing the Mystery of Humanity," Knight-Ridder/Tribune News Service, January 27, 1998.

Peter Kendall and Ronald Kotulak, "Clamor over Cloning" *Chicago Tribune*, January 8, 1998.

Patricia Lefebere, "Cloning Raises Ethical Questions About Life, Human Limits, and Love," *National Catholic Reporter*, March 14, 1997.

Charles Marwick, "Put Human Cloning on Hold, Say Bioethicists," *JAMA*, July 2, 1997.

Michael Mautner, "Will Cloning End Human Evolution?" *Futurist*, November/December 1997.

Bob Messenger, "Cloning: Think of the Possibilities," *Foods Processing*, April 1997.

Oliver Morton, "First Dolly, Now Headless Tadpoles," *Science*, October 31, 1997.

Jim Motavalli and Tracey C. Rembert, "Me and My Shadow," *E*, July/August 1997.

Nicole Noyes, "Why Human Cloning Research Should Not Be Banned," *Cosmopolitan*, October 1997.

Elizabeth Pennisi, "Transgenic Lambs from Cloning Lab: Biotechnology," *Science*, August 1, 1997.

Stephen G. Post, "The Judeo-Christian Case Against Cloning," *America*, June 21, 1997.

Virginia I. Postrel, "Fatalist Attraction: The Dubious Case Against Fooling Mother Nature," *Reason*, July 1997.

Joni Praded, "Cloning: The Missing Debate," *Animals*, May/June 1997.

Pamela Schaeffer, "Cloning Inspires New Talk About the Soul," *National Catholic Reporter*, March 28, 1997.

Joseph Schuman, "19 Nations Agree to Enact Laws That Ban Human Cloning," Associated Press, January 13, 1998.

Harold T. Shapiro, "Ethical and Policy Issues of Human Cloning," *Science*, July 11, 1987.

Sandra Sobieraj, "Clinton Calls Human Cloning Proposal 'Troubling,'" Associated Press, January 11, 1998.

John Stephenson, "Threatened Bans on Human Cloning Research Could Hamper Advances," *JAMA*, April 2, 1997.

Chana Freiman Stiefel, "Cloning: Good Science or Baaaad Idea?" *Science World*, May 2, 1997.

David Stipp, "The Real Biotech Revolution," *Fortune*, March 31, 1997.

"To Clone or Not to Clone?" *Christian Century*, March 19, 1997.

Marian Uhlman, "Plan to Clone Humans a Virtual Minefield," Knight-Ridder News Service, January 8, 1998.

Rebecca Veolker, "A Clone by Any Other Name Is Still an Ethical Concern," *JAMA*, February 2, 1994.

Rick Weiss, "Scientist Plans to Clone a Human a Step Ahead of the Bioethics Cops," *Washington Post*, January 7, 1998.

INDEX

ABOUT THE AUTHOR

Terry O'Neill has a master's degree in American studies and taught high school English and social studies for more than a dozen years. She was an editor for Greenhaven's Opposing Viewpoints, American History, and Great Mysteries series and has both edited and written many other books and magazine articles on subjects ranging from biomedical ethics and adoption rights to ghosts and UFOs. She is the editor in chief of *FATE* magazine.

DATE DUE
